# DILEMMAS OF PUBLIC UNIVERSITY REFORM IN MALAYSIA

# Dilemmas of public university reform in Malaysia

## Machi Sato

Monash University Press
Clayton

Monash University Press
Building 11
Monash University
Victoria 3800, Australia

www.monash.edu.au/mai

All Monash University Press publications are subject to double blind peer review

National Library of Australia cataloguing-in-publication data:


Sato, Machi.

Dilemmas of public university reform in Malaysia.


Bibliography.

ISBN 978 1 87692 441 6.


1. Universities and colleges - Malaysia - Planning. 2. Universities and colleges - Malaysia - Standards. 3. Universities and colleges - Malaysia - Evaluation. I. Title. (Series : Monash papers on Southeast Asia ; no. 63).


378.595


Cover design by Minnie Doron.
Printed by BPA Print Group, Melbourne, Australia - www.bpabooks.com

# contents

## Acknowledgments

I would like first to mention Dr Ian Proudfoot from the Australian National University. It was his attitude towards his profession that convinced me that no-one can establish a good university without good academics. The reputation of the university is built on the effort and passion of individual members of the university community. My thanks also to Dr Molly NN Lee from United Nations Education, Scientific and Cultural Organization Asia and Pacific Regional Bureau for Education for her support and very helpful advice. She was at the Universiti Sains Malaysia when I interviewed her in 2002. Associate Professor Takashi Torii from Meiji University is the one who introduced me to academia and I appreciate the motivation he provided. My special thanks go to my colleagues and friends Aaron Goodman, Chin-Tong Liew, William Edwards, Karyn and Mark, and my family.

This study would not have been possible without the kind co-operation of the many interviewees, who willingly spent time answering my sometimes rather unfocused questions.

Universities are in the midst of a wave of transition in many countries. I do not wish to argue that there is a right or a wrong way forward. Each university must make its own decision about the direction it will take. My hope is that this study will make a small contribution to discussions of university reform.

Machi Sato


## About the author

Machi Sato is a postgraduate student at the Department of Educational Studies, Oxford University. She obtained her MA in Southeast Asian Studies at the Australian National University, where she undertook the research for this publication. Her research interests are higher education in Malaysia and Japan, faculty development, university education, university culture, and the role of academics. Her current research project is on faculty development in Japanese universities.

# Introduction

During the past decade, Malaysia's tertiary education system has experienced a great transformation. In the mid-1990s, legislation was introduced to loosen traditionally tight controls on tertiary education and to democratise and internationalise higher education.[1] A new model for the higher education sector was introduced, as private institutions were allowed to grant degrees and foreign universities were permitted to set up branch campuses in Malaysia. In the past, authority to grant degrees had been strictly limited to public universities.

A further significant reform was the corporatisation of public universities, beginning in 1998. This move aimed to make the curriculum more responsive to the needs of the market and society, as well as to provide greater institutional autonomy. At the same time, public universities, which previously relied on Malay, the national language, as the primary medium of instruction, were requested to begin offering courses in English. Finally, the contentious ethnic quota on admissions to public universities was formally abolished in 2002.[2]

Why have these changes taken place? It is generally accepted that since Malaya's political independence in 1957, its education policy and the roles, functions and organisation of its universities have been predominantly influenced by the nation's economic, political and social development policies.[3] Given the country's multi-ethnic population—in 2001 the population of 23 million was 65% Bumiputera (Malays and other indigenous people), 26% Chinese, 7.7% Indian and 1% from other ethnic groups (JPM 2001:charts 1&2)—the government's greatest challenge has always been to develop a national identity that is acceptable and capable of uniting all ethnic groups. In the past, this was the overriding concern behind the formulation and implementation of education policy in Malaysia. Today the greater emphasis is on the role of universities in producing human resources, as the government steers the production economy towards a knowledge-based economy, otherwise known as a K-economy. In its view, knowledge is the key element needed to survive in the highly competitive, globalised and fast-changing world that arises from the development of science and technology. For this new emphasis, the role of higher education has become crucial.

Malaysians often apply the term 'ivory tower' to the older public universities, reflecting a view that they were a place for the intellectual elite and rather detached from society's needs. This seems less apt today when, as one of the academics I interviewed put it, 'Everyone wants to go to the university and wants a degree' and 'people think education is about acquiring the ability to do a certain thing'. As expectations change, universities' credibility and accountability are questioned. Malaysian universities are better seen, in Selvaratnam's words, as a 'phenomenon interdependent with other parts of society and primarily within the boundaries of the society' (Selvaratnam 1989:203). In this environment, public universities are finding it difficult to keep a balance between market-oriented education and academic values, between responding to the government's control and protecting the institutional autonomy, between responding to social pressure and protecting academic freedom, and between becoming international and staying local.

In the course of my research, I met and interviewed numerous academics from public universities at Malaysian institutions in order to get a first-hand understanding of the processes and implications of public university reform. I consider that, generally speaking, individual academics play a crucial role in developing and maintaining their respective institutions' credibility and reputation. And yet, academics are generally less committed to institutional reform than to their professional bodies or to their disciplines (senior academic, education).[4] Although it may be difficult to encourage academics' active participation in public university reform, without their involvement there can only be ineffective structural changes. In the course of my investigation, it became clear that there was a consensus among academics that public university reform was required and timely; but it was equally clear that reforms were being imposed from above by the government or by the university administration and that academics were rarely consulted or even properly informed about the reform process. Individual institutions were reshaped to reflect wider government policy, and changes seldom came from the grass roots. It therefore remains unclear whether, without the full participation and involvement of academics in the process, the current reforms will actually be improvements.

# Notes

1   Changes are taking place not only in higher education. In 2002 it was decided to teach mathematics and science in English in Primary One, Secondary One and Form Six. The government has also sought to establish what it has called the Vision School, where both national and national-type primary schools will be co-ordinated in order to share resources. By providing an opportunity for primary students to interact at school, the program aims to foster greater understanding and respect among children of different ethnic groups. The idea of the Vision School system was put forward in the Seventh Malaysian Plan (1996–2000). There has been heated discussion and opposition to this plan. The strongest protest came from a Chinese education movement known as Dong Jiao Zong.

2   Nevertheless, entrance requirements are still not standardised, nor based solely on academic merit, allowing an effective quota to be maintained.

3   This idea is common to scholars such as Abd Rahim Abd Rashid (2002), Molly NN Lee (2001a; 2001b), Murray R Thomas (1983), Tan Ai Mei (2001) and Viswanathan Selvaratnam (1989).

4   The degree of academics' loyalty to their universities differs from country to country. See also Boyer, Altbach & Whitelaw (1994).

_chapter one_

# The history of education policy
# and reform in Malaysia

## From independence of Malaya to the 1969 riots[1]

The 'divide and rule' policies, which characterised British colonial rule, facilitated the establishment of an education system suited to British interests (Andaya & Andaya 1982:222–35).[2] Under British control (1874–1946), each of the three principal ethnic groups—Malay, Chinese and Indian—had its own primary schools and used its own language as the medium of instruction. At that time, higher education was a means of creating an elite class among the Malays who would co-operate with the colonial administration. A result of colonial policies and the segmented colonial education system was that when the Federation of Malaya achieved independence in 1957, it faced serious ethnic divisions reinforced by economic and political disparities. The independent government faced a huge challenge in creating a sense of nationhood among the people.

The Constitution of the independent state reflected bargaining between the three major ethnic parties that comprised the ruling alliance. The non-Malay communities were given access to citizenship, in return accepting special provisions that protected Malay interests and identity: making Islam the religion of the Federation and Malay the national language, preserving Malay land rights, preserving the sovereignty, prerogatives and powers of the Malay Rulers, and providing some other specifics that are particularly relevant for education (Suffian 1976:chapter 18). For the establishment of racial harmony and national unity, the leaders drafting the Constitution were convinced that it was necessary for Malays and other indigenous people to play a greater role in the nation's economy. Thus Article 153, which guarantees the 'special position of the Malays', allows the _Yang di-Pertuan Agung_ (King) to reserve places in the public service for Malays and to restrict business licences to Malays: it also allows him to set such proportions of Malays as he may think reasonable for positions in the public service of the Federation; for scholarships, exhibitions and other similar educational or training privileges or special facilities given or accorded by the federal government; and for permits or licenses required by federal law for the operation of any trade or business (Milne & Mauzy 1978:37).

## Higher education until the 1970s

Committees headed by Tun Abdul Razak in 1956 and by Abdul Rahman Talib in 1960 studied the education system and formulated an educational development plan for the nation. The Razak and Talib reports were fundamental in guiding higher education reform in the early years of independence. Both reports emphasised the need to create a new national identity through the education system (Singh & Mukherjee 1993). The Razak report asserted that the 'ultimate objective of education policy…must be to bring together the children of all races under a national educational system in which the national language is the main medium of instruction' (cited in Tham 1979:326). The Talib report similarly emphasised the need to adopt the national language as the main medium of instruction and proposed steps to make Universiti Malaya (UM) a bilingual university, with English and Malay as the medium of instruction (Tham 1979:328).

The Education Act of 1961 became the fundamental law governing education in Malaya. During this period, the government ambitiously sought to create harmonious ethnic relations by using education as a tool, rather than concerning itself with the social and economic benefits that education would potentially provide for society (Hirschman 1979). At this stage the government took only preliminary steps towards restructuring the university, and thus the university itself enjoyed a high level of institutional autonomy (Selvaratnam 1989:196).

UM, the country's first public university, became a separate autonomous university in 1962. UM was formed in British Singapore in 1949 when two British colleges were combined to create an English-medium university.[3] Thus from its earliest days UM was strongly influenced by the British academic and institutional tradition. In 1957, a commission under the chairmanship of Sir Robert Aitken, the Vice-Chancellor of the University of Birmingham, was formed to make recommendations for establishing a new university in Kuala Lumpur. The commission recommended that UM continue to be the only university, but with two autonomous campuses in Singapore and Kuala Lumpur. In 1960, seeing the need for an exclusively national university within its own territorial boundaries, the Federation of Malaya decided to convert the autonomous Kuala Lumpur campus to a fully-fledged university, and in 1962 the former UM became two separate universities, the University of Singapore and the Universiti Malaya (Selvaratnam 1989:188–191). In 1962, UM had only 1341 students and many of its graduates were absorbed into the government sector (Lee 2004:5). It remained Malaya's only university until 1969. As there was an insufficient local pool of scholars, UM was initially staffed largely by expatriate academics (Selvaratnam 1989:195). UM enjoyed a reputation as one of the best higher education institutions in the wider region and staff at UM were very active and passionate in their loyalty to their institution (former academic, education).

In 1962, the Higher Education Planning Committee was formed under the chairmanship of the Minister of Education to develop and improve the higher educational sector. Its report, published in 1967, provided the road map for the creation of new universities in Malaysia. The committee took a vocational view of education, holding that different levels and types of education best prepared students for different types of employment (Snodgrass 1980:252). The committee particularly emphasised the need to expand science education in order to meet the needs of development, recommending that, in the long term, 20% of people within relevant age groups should be provided with facilities for higher education (Malaysia 1967:section 168). To this end, it recommended the establishment of a university college in Penang, which became Universiti Sains Malaysia (USM) in 1969, and the upgrading of the technical college in Kuala Lumpur to become a college of technology. The committee also urged higher education institutions to deliver more courses in the national language. Accepting these recommendations, the government decided to expand higher education, with emphasis on scientific and technical disciplines (Malaysia 1967: section 275–283; Tham 1979:330; Selvaratnam 1989:191–93).

By the mid-1960s there was increasing dissatisfaction among the Malay population with the government's failure to alleviate poverty in Malay communities (Torii 2001:134). In 1966, MARA, *Majlis Amanah Rakyat* or the Trust Council for Indigenous Peoples, was established to improve the social conditions of the Bumiputera. The education and training division of MARA aimed to increase the number of skilled Bumiputera by offering scholarships and loans to Bumiputera students and by setting up educational and training programs.[4] In 1967, Institut Teknologi MARA was established, which would much later, in 1999, become Universiti Teknologi MARA (UTiM).[5]

## The language issue

Article 152 of the 1957 Constitution of the Federation of Malaya established Malay or Bahasa Malaysia as the country's national language, and stated that it must be used for official purposes. However, it also allowed the King to 'permit the continued use of the English language for such official purposes as may be deemed fit' (National Language Act:section 4), and stated that no person may be prohibited from using other languages or from teaching or learning them. The government allotted itself ten years to deal with the national language question. To overcome the deficiencies of Malay in technical terminology and to standardise and upgrade the language, the *Dewan Bahasa dan Pustaka* (Language and Literary Council) was created in 1959 (Mauzy 1985:158). In 1967, the National Language Act confirmed the position of Malay as the sole national language, and required all officially recognised educational programs to be conducted in Malay (Roff 1967). This meant that public universities were required to change their medium of instruction from English to Malay.

This process had hardly begun when the outbreak of severe ethnic riots in 1969 changed the attitude of the government dramatically. It became far more interventionist, implementing radical changes designed to curb the excesses of political competition and to provide a new formula for political rule. In the process, the government took even closer control over education and language policies (Mauzy 1985:157). An emergency administration, known as the National Operations Council, was set up under Tun Abdul Razak's chairmanship, and its first major recommendation was that the Constitution be amended to give parliament the authority to pass laws that:

> [prohibited] the questioning of any matter, right, status, position, privilege, sovereignty or prerogative established or protected by the provisions of Part of the Constitution (Citizenship), Article 152 (the National Language), Article 153 (Special Position of the Malays and the Legitimate Interests of the Other Communities), or Article 181 (the Sovereignty of the Rulers) (Milne & Mauzy 1978:96).

These issues are collectively known as the 'sensitive issues', and by amendment of Articles 63 and 72 they were removed from public debate, even in the parliament.

The National Operations Council concluded that one of the triggers of the conflict between Malays and Chinese was the economic disparity that existed between the two groups. It embarked on an ambitious restructuring of society under the guise of the New Economic Policy (NEP), which would run from 1970 to 1990. The primary objectives of the NEP were stated as the 'eradication of poverty' and 'restructuring society and economic balance' (Milne & Mauzy 1978:326). A key role was reserved for education, especially as a means of targeting the divisive ethnic disparities in employment. The Universities and University Colleges Act (UUCA) of 1971 gave the Ministry of Education full control over all universities in the country. Subsequently, each university had to refer to the ministry on almost all issues, from the creation of new courses to the establishment of new administrative posts.

The government realised that, while sufficient numbers of Bumiputera were getting primary, and to some extent secondary, education, not enough were making the transition to university (Suffian 1976:313). The National Operations Council appointed a committee under the chairmanship of Dr Abdul Majid bin Ismail to report on the student body at UM. His study revealed that in 1968–69, for example, only 1825 out of 5566 students were Malays and that only a small number of them were studying science subjects (Suffian 1976:312–17). In its report to the government, the committee argued:

> the University should state clearly that it is university policy to ensure as far as possible that the racial composition of the student population not only in the University as a whole but on faculty by faculty basis should reflect the racial composition in the country (Tham 1979:334).

This was the basis for the imposition of a 'quota system', which regulated entrance to universities.[6] It was decided that 55% of the places at public universities would be secured for Bumiputera students, and that quotas could be applied to individual faculties and not just to institutions as a whole. A provision empowering the government to implement quotas was included in the amendments to the Federal Constitution in 1971 (Article 153 8A). Besides the quota system, the government vigorously implemented various affirmative action policies, such as awarding scholarships to Bumiputera students and establishing special matriculation courses and colleges exclusively for Bumiputera students.

Throughout the 1970s and 1980s, the government rapidly increased the number of public universities, particularly in rural areas, in order to enable more Bumiputera students to gain access to university. The impact of these positive discrimination policies can be seen in Figure 1, which shows a marked rise in the proportion of Malay or Bumiputera students. Whereas in 1967 they were under-represented on the campus, by 1985 they were over-represented (Ng 1998:99–123).

*Figure 1: Enrolment at universities in Malaysia, by ethnic group, between 1966 and 1985*

| Ethnic group | Total population 1970 | Students at Malaysian universities (%) | | |
|---|---|---|---|---|
| | | 1966-67 | 1970 | 1985 |
| Malay/Bumiputera | 55.5 | 28.8 | 39.7 | 63.0 |
| Chinese | 34.1 | 56.5 | 49.2 | 29.7 |
| Indian & other | 10.4 | 14.7 | 11.1 | 7.3 |
| Total | 100 | 100 | 100 | 100 |

(Department of Statistics 1972:24; Andressen 1993:51; Reid 1988:70)

A result of these affirmative action policies was that the universities lost control of their own admissions, since intake was no longer based on academic merit alone.

The effect of increased government control over the education sector was also evident in the specialisation of several new institutions. In 1969, Universiti Sains Malaysia (USM) was founded, initially offering purely science courses, but later expanding its curriculum to offer arts and education courses. Its goals were to provide for Malaysia's increasing human resources needs in science, industry, social and welfare services, health and education. In 1970, Universiti Kebangsaan Malaysia (UKM) was created, and it was the first university to use Bahasa Malaysia as a medium of instruction in all areas of study.[8] To meet the growing demand for university places, a fourth university, Universiti Pertanian Malaysia (Agricultural University of Malaysia, later Universiti Putra Malaysia (UPM)), was established in the following year by a merger between the Malayan College of Agriculture and the UM's Faculty of Agriculture. Lastly, Institut Teknologi Kebangsaan was upgraded to Universiti Teknologi Malaysia (UTM) in 1975 and offered courses in science and technology (Ministry of Education 2001a:71; Lee 2004). As Lee observes:

> the expansion saw the Ministry of Education playing a dominant role in planning and coordinating the development of university programmes so as to avoid the duplication of courses of study in these different universities unless there were convincing reasons that this was necessary. Therefore, each of the newly established universities had an area of focus in their fields of specialization (Lee 2004:6).

The government's control also extended to controlling students' activities. As the number of universities increased, more students from rural and poor families obtained tertiary places. Those students, getting involved with student bodies, began to raise issues relating to the lives of the people, especially the poor peasants (Crouch 1996:92–93; Hassan & Hamid 1984:1–3; Funston 1980:278–281). On 29 August 1969, police invaded the UM campus to break up a demonstration against the Prime Minister and detained several students. This was the first time that the police had ventured on to the campus, and it was considered by students to be a violation of university autonomy.

As the number of universities and higher learning institutions increased in the 1970s, with most located around Kuala Lumpur, the government began to fear a growing student movement hostile to government policies. In December 1974, a demonstration to support the struggle of peasants proved a turning point. Thousands of student demonstrators took to the streets demanding immediate steps against corruption. As a result, some 1169 students and others were arrested, along with the then leader of the Malaysian Islamic Youth Movement,

Anwar Ibrahim. In the wake of these demonstrations, the then Minister of Education, Dr Mahathir Mohamad, reacted forcefully by imposing restrictions on scholarship-holders and amending the UUCA. The 1975 amendments to the UUCA prohibited students from joining or 'allying themselves' with political parties, trade unions, or 'any other organization, body or other group' without the written permission of the Vice-Chancellor (Crouch 1996:93). All student organisations were dissolved and, instead, the government set up Student Representative Councils (Hassan & Hamid 1984:10–18). Members of the academic staff, and administrative staff, or officers of the university, were also prohibited from holding office in political parties and, because they were now classed as public servants, the Official Secrets Act and the Printing Presses and Publication Act were also available to regulate their publications and public statements.

## Merdeka University

While reforms to higher education clearly favoured Bumiputera students, non-Bumiputera communities were left almost powerless. One issue in particular, namely the campaign for the creation of Merdeka University (Independence University), illustrates the inability of non-Bumiputera to affect educational policies.

The idea of creating a Chinese-medium university, known as Merdeka University, was first floated by the Chinese Guilds and Chambers of Commerce in 1967, when Malay was confirmed as Malaysia's official language. It was a reaction to a perceived denial of educational opportunities to Chinese in public universities and colleges (Tham 1979:348). The issue was heatedly debated in the 1969 election, with all Chinese-based opposition parties declaring their support for the establishment of a Chinese-language university (Reid 1988:68–74). However, the outbreak of the race riots that followed the election quickly put an end to the Merdeka University campaign. It was not until 1978 that the proposal was revived, to become an issue in the 1978 election. The Minister of Education, Datuk Musa Hitam, firmly opposed it on three grounds. First, by using Chinese as the medium of instruction, Merdeka University would breach the National Language Act of 1967, which stated that Bahasa Malaysia must be the medium of instruction in all public institutions (Roff 1967). Second, it would be a private university, which was prohibited by the UUCA. Third, it would be divisive, as it would cater solely to ethnic Chinese (Tham 1979:348).

The failure of the Merdeka University proposal is indicative of the increasing lack of political power of non-Bumiputera (Andressen 1998:65), as well as the government's insistence on retaining tight control over higher education in order to shape the process of nation-building.

## The failure of the NEP model for higher education

After being elected as Prime Minister in 1981, Mahathir introduced a series of plans to accelerate development. His three major initiatives in the early 1980s were the establishment of the Heavy Industry Corporation of Malaysia, the concept of Malaysia Incorporated and the policy of privatisation. The impact of these plans was to create more demand for skilled workers and, as previously, the universities' role was to generate the required human resources. The heavy industry policy, which required substantial government subsides, soon faced difficulties due to the economic recession that began in 1985. As a result, the emphasis shifted, and implementation of the privatisation policy was accelerated (Crouch 1996:227).

In 1985, the Economic Planning Unit of the Prime Minister's Department issued its *Guidelines on privatisation*, which outlined policy aims, modes of privatisation and means of implementation (Jomo 1994:261). The guidelines set out the five objectives of privatisation: relieving the financial burden on government; reducing the size and presence of government; accelerating growth through private investment in the economy; promoting competition and raising efficiency and productivity; and meeting the equity or distributional objectives of government (EPU 1991).

There were two principal reasons behind Mahathir's support for privatisation. He believed that the profit-seeking private sector had an incentive to 'deliver the goods', which was lacking in the government sector. As Jomo (1994:266) explains, 'Privatised entities are...expected to find themselves in competitive markets or environments. Competition generally encourages more efficient behaviour among private (as well as public) entities or companies in order to achieve both productive and allocative efficiencies.' Mahathir also saw the privatisation policy as an ideal vehicle for achieving one of the aims of the NEP, which was to increase business ownership by Bumiputera (Milne & Mauzy 1978:56–58). Training institutions such as Institut Teknologi MARA had been boosted in order to provide Malays with the necessary business skills (Milne & Mauzy 1978:330), but most graduating trainees were employed in state organisations, many of which were not efficiently run and tended to absorb excess human resources. As state-run organisations were privatised, more Malays would participate in running business enterprises, and that would lead to a more balanced ethnic distribution of employment in all sectors and at all levels (Milne & Mauzy 1978:56–57). In line with the concept of Malaysia Incorporated, modelled on Japan Incorporated, the private and public sectors were encouraged to work closely together to achieve the nation's prosperity. To facilitate this, the government undertook greater deregulation, simplified administrative procedures and provided better incentives, which led to the strengthening of the private sector's contribution to economic growth (Tan 2001:11).

The definitions and methods of privatisation are numerous. In the Malaysian context, privatisation covers the corporatisation of public utilities, the sale of public enterprises and the awarding of licenses to private enterprises to permit them to participate in activities previously the exclusive preserve of the public sector (Jomo 1994:265). By the late 1990s, privatisation had been applied in various forms to previously state-run activities such as airlines, airports, shipping, telecommunications, roads and so on. However, when the policy was initiated in the mid-1980s, no particular attention was given to the public universities.

In the early 1980s, the government had set up two more state universities, Universiti Islam Antarabangsa Malaysia (International Islamic University of Malaysia (UIAM)) in 1983[9] and Universiti Utara Malaysia (University of Northern Malaysia) in 1984.[10] However, the delivery of higher education by private institutions was beginning to expand. By the mid-1980s, the NEP model for the higher education system was experiencing stress from several directions. Because of quota restrictions on admissions to public universities for non-Malay students, the number of Malaysian students studying in overseas institutions had been increasing since the 1970s. By 1980, there were 21,994 students enrolled at local universities (Awang 1994:105), while 39,908 Malaysian students were studying at overseas universities, of whom 60.5% were Chinese, 23% Malays, 15.9% Indians and 0.6% other Malaysians (*Education Quarterly* 2000:14–20). Then, with the global recession of the mid-1980s and the imposition of full fees on overseas students by the United Kingdom and Australian governments, it became harder for Malaysian families to send children overseas. As a result, the demand for local higher educational institutions rose to unprecedented levels. To meet this demand, by the mid-1980s many private colleges started to offer degree programs in conjunction with partner universities, principally in the United Kingdom. Such arrangements came to be known as 'twinning programs'[11], and allowed students to complete one or two years in Malaysia before proceeding to the twinning partner institution overseas for the remainder of the program to complete the degree.[12]

By acquiescing in the delivery of higher education by private institutions, the government allowed the number of places available to expand rapidly. However, until the amendment of the UUCA in 1995 and the introduction of the Private Higher Education Institutions Act in 1996, there was no legislation to regulate private institutions, and the government was no longer able to maintain its strict control over the full gamut of higher education institutions.

## The rise of private institutions

In 1990, the National Development Plan (NDP) replaced the NEP as the country's fundamental development plan. The NDP restated the NEP's aims; however, the new emphasis was less on the distribution of wealth and more on the rapid development of an active Bumiputera commercial and industrial community (Milne & Mauzy 1999:72–73; Torii 2001:135). In 1991, Mahathir presented a new development philosophy, entitled *Malaysia: the way forward*, also known as Vision 2020, which underpinned the NDP. Vision 2020 stresses the need for political stability, the promotion of industrialisation, and growth in business and technology in order to bolster economic development, enhance national unity and reduce poverty. Mahathir also emphasised the role of the education system in producing a healthy human resource base as a key to the country's development. The plan states that 'nothing is more important than the development of human resources...Our people is our ultimate resource' (Mahathir 1991). Thus, one of the foremost goals of the plan was to enrich the country's human resource base, which the government recognised as fundamental if Malaysia was to compete with other countries in the world economy.

For the first five years of the NDP, very few changes were made to education policies. The government set up two more public universities in East Malaysia, Universiti Malaysia Sarawak in 1992 and Universiti Malaysia Sabah in 1994, but these made an insignificant contribution to meeting the demand for increased access to higher education.

In 1994, as part of the ultimate phase of the country's industrialisation program, the Multimedia Super Corridor project was conceived (Milne & Mauzy 1999:76). The Multimedia Super Corridor is an 'information superhighway' designed to facilitate the development of information technology as the next engine of growth for Malaysia and to make Malaysia an information technology hub in the region. In 1996, over 30 world-ranking computer and information technology (IT) companies signed up to participate in the project, located south of Kuala Lumpur. Naturally, this has caused a greater demand for skilled IT workers. Competition among Southeast Asian countries for the most qualified IT workers had already created a shortage of workers in this leading industry in Malaysia. Many IT workers trained in Malaysia had moved to the United States and Singapore for more lucrative salaries, while Malaysia began to import IT workers from countries such as India. Yet the *Far Eastern Economic Review* estimated that Malaysia would require another 15,000 IT workers by the end of 2000. This became another trigger for the expansion of private higher educational institutions. The number of new private higher education institutions concentrating on IT education grew throughout the 1990s (*FEER* 2000).

Meanwhile, the public universities were slow to respond to these changes, despite the increasing social pressure on them to be more sensitive and responsive to the needs of the economy. The important role of private higher education institutions in complementing public institutions became increasingly evident, as they were acknowledged for their contribution towards producing the semi-professional and managerial personnel needed to meet the new demands of the changing economy (Tan 2001:10). Between 1985 and 1995, the number of students enrolled in private higher education institutions jumped from 15,000 to 127,594, while the number of students in public institutions only increased from 86,330 to 189,020 (Tan 2001:tables 5&6). By the early 1990s, there were hundreds of non-degree private colleges and dozens of private colleges offering foreign universities' degrees, none of which fell under government jurisdiction.

In order to deal with this rapidly evolving situation, the government enacted a major revision of its education policies. In late 1995, the Minister of Education, Najib bin Tun Abdul Razak shepherded a package of five bills through parliament (*Asiaweek* 1996). Two bills made extensive amendments to the existing Education Act and the UUCA, and were intended to enable higher educational institutions to cater for increasing and changing demands. In January 1995, the vice-chancellors of public universities had met to discuss a paper by the new Vice-Chancellor of UM, Dr Abdullah Sanusi, proposing the corporatisation of UM and the University Hospital. The report of the meeting was then submitted to the government's Economic Planning Unit, and it was decided that public universities would be corporatised in the near future (Loh 1996:2–8). As a consequence, the amended UUCA gave greater administrative and financial autonomy to public universities, laying the groundwork for all the public universities to be corporatised. The implementation of this policy will be discussed in more detail in chapter three.

The three remaining new Acts targeted the orderly development of private higher education. These were the Private Higher Educational Institutions Act, the National Council of Higher Education Act, and the National Accreditation Board Act.[13] Provisions in the Private Higher Educational Institutions Act forced private colleges to register with the government, and the curriculum and instruction offered by each registered college began to be examined by the National Council.

Malaysia has seen a further mushrooming of numbers and varieties of private higher education institutions since 1996. In 2003, there were 11 private universities, four foreign branch campuses and some 600 private colleges with various programs including twinning, franchised international programs, distance learning, open/virtual learning, local university franchise programs and so on.[14] The dominant players responsible for setting up private universities are large corporations and organisations closely linked with the government, such as Telekom Malaysia Berhad, Tenaga Nasional Berhad and Petronas. Political parties of the Barisan Nasional government have also sponsored the establishment of universities, such as the Malayan (later Malaysian) Chinese Association's (MCA) Universiti Tunku Abdul Rahman and United Malay National Organization's (UMNO) Universiti Tun Abdul Razak. Three different bodies have emerged to represent private institutions, namely, the National Council of Private and Independent Educational Institutions (NAPIEI), the Malaysian Association of Private Colleges and Universities (MAPCU), and Gabungan Institusi Pendidikan Tinggi Swasta Bumiputera (GIPTSB) or the Union of Malay Private Higher Education Institutions. NAPIEI is the oldest association, representing small and medium-sized private colleges, while MAPCU represents the larger private colleges. GIPTSB represents 100 Malay private colleges, concerning itself mainly with their sustainability. These Malay colleges were established in order to deliver courses franchised by the public universities (Tan 2001:chapters 5&6), but, in general, the private colleges' curriculum place greater emphasis on science, technology, engineering and other technology-based subjects. They also offer a wider variety of programs than most foreign educational institutions.

## The business of education

Malaysia's economy enjoyed high growth through the 1990s until the Asian financial crisis struck in August 1997. Gross domestic product growth reached 9.5% in 1995 and 8.2% in 1996 (Milne & Mauzy 1999:74). The unemployment rate was as low as 2.9% in 1995, which meant virtually full employment. In an unprecedented move to ease labour shortages and to move young people into jobs faster, the government decided to shorten university courses from four to three years, beginning in 1996 (*Reuters News* 1995).

Meanwhile, the number of public universities has steadily increased as former colleges have been upgraded. In 1999, Kolej Universiti Sains dan Teknologi Malaysia (Malaysian University College of Science and Technology) and Kolej Universiti Terengganu (Terengganu University College) were set up, followed by Kolej Universiti Teknikal Kebangsaan Malaysia (National Technical University College of Malaysia) and Kolej Universiti Teknologi Tun Hussein Onn (Tun Hussein Onn University College of Technology) in 2001. By 2003, there was a total of 18 public universities.

The government and the private sector have come to recognise higher education as a potentially profitable new service. Large numbers of Malaysian students continue to study overseas. In 1996, for example, approximately 50,000 students were studying abroad and this was draining about AUS$1 billion a year from Malaysia's foreign exchange. From this experience, the Malaysian government understands very well that people are willing to spend large amounts of money on their children's education, and that the education business could prove a reliable source of income. In 1994, the then Minister of Education, Datuk Dr Sulaiman Daud, claimed that amendments to the Education Acts would 'enable [the government] to develop education as a significant component of the service industry and to eventually internationalise and develop it as a service export' (*New Straits Times* 1994). Daud and others in government judged that supplying education could yield numerous positive financial and other benefits.

Private higher educational institutions have the potential to attract students from overseas countries such as Indonesia, China, Thailand, and several Arab and African countries. The diversity of languages and religions current in Malaysia, its moderate cost of living, and the availability of various twinning program with higher education institutions from Western countries would all attract students from overseas. Indeed, the number of international students is growing, especially since the Asian financial crisis in 1997, which provided an added impetus for Malaysia's private higher education institutions to recruit international students. Students from neighbouring countries, as well as other developing countries, began to choose Malaysia as the destination for tertiary education when the currencies of their home countries lost value, making it too costly to send their children to Western countries such as Australia, the United States or the United Kingdom. Since 1997, the Malaysian government has led a number of 'education road-shows' to countries in the region (Tan 2001:181). In 2003, the Minister of Education, Tan Sri Musa Mohamad, stated that Malaysia aims to double the number of international students studying in Malaysia to 50,000 by 2010.[15] To achieve this goal, education promotion centres were to be opened in Jakarta, Ho Chi Minh City, Dubai and Beijing by the end of 2003 (Liew 2003). Also in 2003, the Deputy Minister of Education led a Malaysian delegation consisting of officials from the Department of Private Education and representatives from Malaysian higher education institutions, including UM and USM, on an 11-day promotional tour to China (Chia 2003).[16]

For the government, there may be strategic benefits in developing educational links with developing countries. Those who study in Malaysia learn about their host country in great depth. It would, moreover, enhance Malaysia's claim to a leadership role among developed nations, especially in promoting South–South co-operation in a practical way that allows a move away from dependence on wealthier Northern nations.[17] In the process, Malaysia would benefit by gaining an enormous market and creating local employment, as well as achieving greater influence in international relations. For Malaysian companies, investment in education can be similarly profitable but also a wise public relations move (interview with Nina Adlan 26.9.2000) The *Far Eastern Economic Review* commented:

> Education, if well-conceived, organized and administered, can add mileage to business in several ways: identification as a business contribution to social responsibility to attract goodwill and in building relationships, generation of spin-offs such as recruitment, training, and staff development, research and consultancy to benefit the business and contributing to cash flow, as education is largely transacted on a cash basis (Chin 1994).

However, the idea of making Malaysia the education hub for the region brings back to centre stage the questions of language of instruction and ethnic participation rates. As most private institutions run programs in co-operation with foreign institutions, their main medium of instruction is English. Also, if those institutions are to attract international students (other than from Indonesia), inevitably they have to use English. As a result, public institutions teach in the Malay language and private institutions teach in English. Among domestic students, private institutions mostly cater to non-Malays, especially Chinese, reviving political concerns about an ethnic imbalance in higher education.[18]

## After the Asian financial crisis

The Asian financial crisis in 1997 derailed the nation's political and economic development plans. Confronting the crisis, the government permitted the introduction of '3+0' programs, which would allow Malaysian students to complete foreign universities' degrees without having to go overseas. Additionally, the government decided not to follow its plan to cut the funding of public universities, despite the fact that they had been corporatised. At the same time, unemployment among graduates of public universities began be an issue.

In April 2000 graduates accounted for up to 15% of Malaysia's unemployed (*New Straits Times* 2000).[19] The Unemployed Graduate Retraining Scheme was introduced together with the Retrenched Workers Training Scheme in November 2001 to provide three to six months training, paying graduates in this scheme Malaysian ringgit (RM) 500 per month. In 2002, 10,000 fresh graduates were unemployed and RM100 million was allocated to retrain 15,000 unemployed graduates in 2003 (Lam 2003; Kaur 2003). As the percentage of unemployed grew, questions about the quality of education at public universities were asked, especially concerning the disparity between industry demands and the available number of skilled workers. In order to improve the situation, the government decided to introduce quality assurance measures. Thus, the Division of Quality Assurance was set up within the Higher Education Department in the Ministry of Education in 2001.

Regardless of the graduate unemployment issue, demand for places in public institutions kept growing. In response, in 1999, the government announced the establishment of a consortium of 11 public universities, the Multimedia Technology Enhancement Operations (METEOR) Sdn. Bhd, Sendrian Berhad., to focus on the development and use of multimedia technology to offer distance learning.[20] The two missions of METEOR are to advance the development of information and communications technology and related applications in all aspects of society; and to design, develop and deliver high quality multimedia-based learning programs.[21] By 2001, METEOR had introduced 25 courses in areas such as multimedia, law, business and humanities, benefiting approximately 20,000 students (Malaysia 2001:104).

The most recent phase of the government's development plan is embodied in the ten-year Third Outline Perspective Plan (OPP3) for 2001 to 2010 and the current five-year plan, the Eighth Malaysia Plan, for the period 2000 to 2005. The Eighth Malaysia Plan is designed to overcome the downturn caused by the economic crisis of 1997 to 1998, while the OPP3 embodies the National Vision Policy (NVP). The NVP has taken over the primary objectives of the NEP and the NDP, and is guided by Vision 2020.[22] The NVP supports the development of a knowledge-based economy, both to enhance productivity and to deal with a rapidly changing global environment. It observes that the 'Malaysian economy will face greater challenges as a result of increasing globalization and liberalization as well as the rapid development of technology, especially information and communications technology' (Malaysia 2001:chapter one). Budget increases are proposed to achieve education reform, and the education sector will be kept under review so that it continues to support Malaysia's human resource development: '[E]fforts will be undertaken to develop an efficient and responsive education and training system to meet the demand for a knowledgeable and highly skilled labour force that is equipped with positive values and attitudes' (Malaysia 2001:chapter one).

The government emphasises research and development, especially in mathematics and science. Recently, the executive director of the National Economic Action Council, Mustapa Mohamed, proposed the creation of a world-class 'super' university with the best students and academicians (Leong 2003). The idea was rejected by the Minister of Education, Tan Sri Musa Mohamad, in favour of spreading research funding across existing universities (*Star online* 2003b). Currently UM, USM and UKM are recognised as research universities, but discussion of a 'super' university continues. This debate at least reflects the government's continuing emphasis on a knowledge-based economy and investment in education.

English proficiency has also been given full priority. Reflecting this emphasis, it was decided to teach mathematics and science instruction in English starting in Primary One, Secondary One and Form Six beginning in 2003. According to the Eighth Malaysia Plan, the participation of the private sector at the tertiary level will be intensified and universities, both private and public, will be encouraged to develop centres of excellence comparable with those in reputable foreign universities.[23]

Finally, a significant policy change took place in 2001 when Mahathir announced that there would no longer be an ethnic quota on admission to public universities. Henceforth, student intake would be based solely on the results of either *Sijil Tinggi Persekolahan Malaysia* (STPM) or a matriculation course. STPM is an exam taken after a two-year course in Form Six, while the matriculation course is an in-house one-year course for Bumiputera students. As Figure 2 shows, under the new arrangements the ethnic ratio was kept reasonably balanced, even with the lifting of quotas.

*Figure 2: Enrolment at public universities in Malaysia, by ethnic group, 2002 and 2003*

|  | 2002 | | 2003 | |
|---|---|---|---|---|
| Bumiputera | 22,557 | (68.9%) | 23,182 | (62.6%) |
| Chinese | 8,665 | (26.4%) | 11,921 | (32.2%) |
| Indian | 1,530 | (4.7%) | 1,931 | (5.2%) |
| Total | 32,752 | | 37,034 | |

(JPM 2001)

The continuing balance has allowed the government to talk comfortably about a meritocracy system. However, some political parties and educationalists have questioned whether meritocracy really applies, given the different standards used to assess students entering university on the two pathways.

## Conclusion

Changes in the structure of higher education in Malaysia have generally taken place as a reaction to changes in the economic or political environment, and initially came about by government directive. However, ever-increasing involvement in the global economy and internationalised society has pushed the government to liberalise its policies, and consequently recent reforms in higher education have decentralised higher education, giving more administrative autonomy to educational institutions. At the same time, understanding the importance of education policies in the nation's overall development framework, the government still endeavours to design the education environment and supervise education developments.

# Notes

1   In 1957, British rule ended and the Federation of Malaya was established. In 1963 it joined with Sabah, Sarawak and Singapore to become the Federation of Malaysia. In 1965 Singapore became separate nation.

2   For more on the development of education during the pre-independence period, refer to Loh (1975).

3   The colleges were the King Edward VII College of Medicine and the Raffles College. The King Edward VII College of Medicine was founded in 1904 to train students in the professions of medicine, dentistry and pharmacy. The Raffles College, founded in 1928, provided courses in English, history, mathematics, physics, chemistry, biology and geography. Most of the graduates became teachers and a small number of Malays were recruited into the Malay Administrative Service and Malayan Civil Service. For more on the impact of the British university model, see Selvaratnam (1989:187–205).

4   The predecessor of MARA is the Rural and Industrial Development Authority or RIDA, which was also concerned with the problem of Malay poverty (Gale 1981: chapter three).

5   It was established as an experimental centre in 1956, which was renamed MARA College in 1965. In 1967, MARA College was again renamed Institut Teknologi MARA.

6   The International Islamic University has a separate set of admission criteria.

7   In 1966 and 1967, UM was the only university in Malaysia.

8   The idea of establishing such a university was first mooted as early as the 1920s. However, the British did not favour the idea.

9   The mediums of instruction at UIAM were English and Arabic.

10   UIAM was a pet project of Mahathir, and it attempted to integrate Islamic values with contemporary professional education. Its academic programs focused on management, accountancy, economics, public administration and so on. Its mediums of instruction were English and Arabic.

11   For in-depth study of the development of private higher education institutions, see Tan (2001).

12   Many non-Malay former public university lecturers were involved with the establishment and running of private higher education institutions. The most successful and well-known private institution run by a former non-Malay academic is the HELP (Higher Education Learning Program) University College that was established by Dr Paul Chan, a former academic in the Faculty of Economics and Administration, UM.

13   The Education Act and the UUCA were revised in 1995 and the Private Higher Educational Institutions Act and the National Council of Higher Education Act were brought into force in 1996.

14   Refer to Appendix I for information on the different forms of courses delivered at private higher education institutions.

15  The speech was given at the Malaysia Education Summit 2003. There were then 28,024 international students in Malaysia.

16  The Deputy Minister of Education was Hon Choon Kin.

17  The Foreign Ministry's website explained Malaysia's leadership potential thus: 'Being less dependent on foreign aid and assistance, Malaysia has been able to speak up on issues that other developing countries feel constrained to voice for fear of retribution by the major, particularly western, powers' (www.kln.gov.my).

18  'A major disparity between the two types of institutions is the student composition. It is clear that private colleges and universities are becoming the domain of urban Chinese and Indians with only a handful of Malays and those from Sabah and Sarawak...This ethnic mix is also reflected in staffing. Thus we see a lopsided scenario, which indeed speaks loud on a number of issues, importantly raising the question, why are the rich losing faith in the old ivory towers?' (Khattab 2002).

19  Figures are from the Ministry of Human Resources.

20  The 11 universities are UM, USM, UKM, UPM, UTM, UTiM, Universiti Utara Malaysia, University Malaysia Sabah (UMS), Universiti Malaysia Sarawak (UNIMAS), Universiti Pendidikan Sultan Idris and Universiti Islam Antarabangsa Malaysia (UIAM).

21  Information available at www.meteor.com.my/.

22  The new dimensions of the NVP are as follows: developing Malaysia into a knowledge-based society; generating endogenously-driven growth through strengthening domestic investment and developing national capability, while continuing to attract foreign direct investment in strategic areas; increasing the dynamism of agriculture, manufacturing and services sectors through greater infusion of knowledge; addressing pockets of poverty in remote areas and among Orang Asli and Bumiputera minorities in Sabah and Sarawak, as well as increasing the income and quality of life of those in the lowest 30% by 2010; increasing the participation of Bumiputera in the leading sectors of the economy; and re-orientating human resource development to support a knowledge-based society (Mahathir 2001).

23  The OPP3 also discusses lifelong learning and proposes the establishment of community colleges (Mahathir 2001).

*chapter two*

# University transformation: international perspectives and Malaysia's case

Public university reform is a common phenomenon across the industrialised countries. Interestingly, regardless of differences in social, economic and political conditions, the shape and direction of the reform tends to be similar. The 'ivory tower' is replaced by the 'enterprise university' (Marginson & Considine 2000), the 'knowledge factory' (Aronowitz 2000) and the 'entrepreneurial university' (Clark 1998). Malaysia, though still a developing country, has recently introduced similar public university reforms.

This chapter outlines various models and theories of university reform, which have been deduced by examining trends in American and European universities. With the benefit of these models and theories, I will attempt to locate Malaysia's public universities on a broader mapping of the evolution of universities, and will consider how far the same models and theories can be used to understand Malaysia's own education reforms.

## Models

In his 1963 study, *The uses of the university*, Clark Kerr describes three models of the university. Traditionally the university was 'a community of masters and students' and its purpose was to educate a 'universal liberal man' (Kerr 1995:chapter one). The first universities had the form of a guild of members of the same profession. For an apposite statement of the nature of the traditional university, Kerr points to John Henry Newman's *The idea of a university*, published in 1852.[1] For Newman, the university is 'a place of teaching universal knowledge…[whose] object is, on the one hand, intellectual not moral; and on the other…it is the diffusion and extension of knowledge rather than the advancement' (Newman 1976:4). Traditional universities in this mould were more or less autonomous, generally small and stable, and had considerable control over their own destinies. His second model is the modern university, which emerged as early as 1930 as institutions became more specialised, with departments and faculties devoted to specific fields of study. This arrangement enabled scholars to pursue more specialised education and research, and to emerge as highly qualified specialists in an academic field (Kerr 1995:chapter one). In some countries, especially in the United States, a third model has evolved: the 'multiversity', which functions as everything from a research centre to a vocational training institution, a teacher-training school, a business school and so forth. Providing services for the general public is an important function of this kind of university. For faculty members, two new job titles come into vogue, namely, 'consultant' and 'administrator', which are beyond the traditional roles of researcher and lecturer. Such changes make teaching less central than it was in the older models (Kerr 1995:31–33).

Universities can be thought of as combining elements of one or more of these three models. Kerr observed that each has its own followers. The idea of the traditional university tends to be espoused by the humanists and the generalists, with an emphasis on undergraduate education. The scientists and the specialists put more emphasis on specialised education and the university they aspire to is the modern university. The administrators and the leadership groups in society at large tend to favour the concept of the multiversity (Kerr 1995:7). In industrialised countries today, universities lean toward the modern university or the multiversity, which are seen as efficient and responsive to change.

## Transitions of higher education

A dynamic framework for describing structural changes to the university was first proposed by Martin Trow, a professor of Sociology of Education, in 1972 and has gained wide international acceptance. According to Trow's scheme, universities in industrial countries are in transition as they move from elite higher education through mass higher education and to universal access higher education. As the university transforms itself, moving from one stage of higher education to another, which Trow calls the 'phase transition', there will be strains and tensions, which in turn give rise to the search for new forms and solutions (Trow 1986:66).

Trow uses the percentage of student population among the age cohort of 17–22 as the yardstick to categorise the stages of higher education. Elite higher education has 1–15% of the age cohort of 17–22 as student population, mass higher education has 15–50% and universal access higher education has more than 50%. Each stage implies a different character of education and different forms for the higher education institutions.

Within social elites it is considered a privilege to receive a higher education, the purpose of which is to develop future leaders. For example in the United States, a favoured form of higher educational institution is a liberal arts college.

Universal access higher education gives opportunity to all, at first only to those in the age cohort 17–22, but then, as it develops, the opportunity is extended to all people regardless of age. The result is an institution that offers higher education and lifelong education to the public. The ultimate stage of universal access higher education is universal attendance, where almost everyone receives some kind of higher education.

*Figure 3: Transitions of higher education according to Trow*

| Types of higher education system | Elite | Mass | Universal access |
|---|---|---|---|
| % of student age population | 1–15% | 15–50% | 50%+ |
| Countries (example) | Parts of Europe | Japan, Canada, Sweden | United States |
| Access to higher education | Limited access to higher education; privilege | Limited to people who meet certain requirements | Open opportunities for the population at large |
| Purpose of eduction | Educate the elite | Educate specialists | Universal and lifelong education |

(Trow 1972)

The structural strains created in the 'phase transition' produce problems in areas surrounding the university's function and standards, staffing, admission and finance. Resolving these generally requires university reform (Trow 1986:78). Trow explains that when the student population rises, the average age at which the young start working is delayed. At the same time, government spending on education increases, which means the taxpayers' burden also rises. The expansion of higher education also means that higher education degrees lose their exclusiveness, disappointing many of the educated as they lose their prestige (UNESCO 1998:20). Due to these changes, the public begins to question the benefit and purpose of having people educated in tertiary institutions. As a result, universities increasingly come under pressure to demonstrate their accountability and relevance for the social, economic or political activities of their respective national communities.[2]

## The rise of student consumerism

From a vantage point later in the 1980s, observing the great transformation of America's universities through the 1960s and 1970s as the rapidly expanding student population took universities into the era of mass higher education, David

Riesman highlighted the transition from the principle of 'academic merit' to that of 'student consumerism'. In his analysis, the dominant features of this transition include the decline of faculty influence and the new supremacy of the student market (Riesman 1968, cited in Kitamura 2001:140–47). Students became customers receiving academic service in the 'academic supermarket', which affected, for instance, the design of curriculum and teaching methods. Riesman asserted that students emerged as passive customers whose aim was to obtain academic certificates and that, therefore, ironically, the students tend to become involuntary captives of the institution.

Trow discusses this in terms of the students' involuntary attendance. As higher education moves from mass to universal access higher education, many students are not fully committed to their own education. In Trow's words, they 'really do not want to be in college, have not entered into willing contract with it, and do not accept the values or legitimacy of the institution'. He sees this as fuelling student pressures against formal course requirements and grades. As a result, in order to 'turn the student on', the university puts more emphasis on flexibility and relevance in the curriculum, placing less dependence on books and reading and more dependence on fieldwork and contemporary experience (Trow 1986:70).

These impacts of student consumerism have been compounded by demographic change. Currently, American universities face a declining youth population. The resulting competition among universities to attract students has created conditions that favour student consumerism, as universities fear losing income from tuition fees. As students tend to be vocationally minded, stronger 'student consumerism' tends to lead to courses becoming more market-oriented (Interview with Don Anderson 22.5.2003).[3]

## Accountability

One of the factors motivating the expansion of higher education is the rising demand for skilled human resources as the global economy shifts from a mass production base to ever more specialised industries in the knowledge economy. The design of curriculum, courses and research has been greatly affected by pressure from the world of work. Universities are expected to produce specialised and skilled human resources capable of competing in the international market (OECD 1987). As the UNESCO World Conference on Higher Education in 1998 concluded:

> The more higher education expands, the more knowledge becomes a key factor of productivity, and the more global competition intensifies, the more institutions

of higher education are expected to regard communication and cooperation with the world of work as a means of improving the education provided as well as the employment opportunities of their student (UNESCO 1998:20).

The rise of student consumerism, the increasing burden of higher education on taxpayers, and an appreciation of the economic benefits of investment in higher education have combined to produce demands for greater accountability by universities to the wider society. Budget constraints mean that both governments and the universities are struggling to find ways of efficiently utilising limited resources; thus, there is a need to determine priorities. The result is greater scrutiny and emphasis on the evaluation of courses and programs, assessment of student and institutional performance, and quality assurance. So, quality assurance also becomes an issue as a result of mass higher education, as noted by Molly Lee (2002b:4) when she quotes Brennan and Shah (2000):

> In the past when the higher education system was small and elitist, it could rest its claim to quality and excellence on selectivity, that is, only the best' were admitted as students and only the most able were allowed to teach them.

Once this filtering is no longer in place, the search begins for indicators of quality assurance, which will certify that the university is contributing to the public good and the nation's overall prosperity.

Burton Clark (1998:13) characterises the complexity of the situation facing today's universities as follows:

> Pushed and pulled by enlarging, interacting streams of demand, universities are pressured to change their curricula, alter their faculties, and modernize their increasingly expensive physical plant and equipment—and to do so more rapidly than ever.

According to William Cummings (1998), the demand for the traditional activities of universities has peaked and today society is interested in new types of knowledge products, relative to those traditionally supplied by universities. At the same time, there are new competitors, other than the established universities, that are asserting their ability to supply these products.

## The idea of isomorphism

Scholars seem to agree that these pressures have produced similar patterns of university reform in various countries over the last three decades (Dill & Sporn 1995:chapter one). Strengthened institutional leadership has been a common response by universities striving to stimulate innovation and entrepreneurship (Cummings 1998:200). Organisational theorist James Bess (1988:12) describes the impact of the new demands:

colleges and universities are constrained toward 'pure' bureaucracy or 'organizational rationality' in the interest of stabilizing the internal decision-making process, while at the same time they are pressured toward loose structures that are more readily responsive and adaptive to external conditions...

This desired mix of strengthened leadership and responsive flexibility has seemed to be provided by corporatisation.

Corporatisation is the process of transforming a state body into an independent commercial company. It is often the first stage of a process of privatisation, where ownership of a former state body is ultimately transferred to private individuals and institutional investors through the floating of shares and subsequent listing on a stock exchange (Bostock 1998). The process of privatisation may stop at the stage of corporatisation in areas that the government does not wish to be run wholly as businesses, such as health and education. The corporatisation of health and education generally occurs late in the privatisation process (Salazar 2004).[4]

The aim of corporatisation is to improve quality, productivity and efficiency. Its main characteristics are that it gives more autonomy to an institution in administration and management; it reduces the government's public expenditure; and the government's status changes from state control to a state supervisory role. Corporate governance conforms with the system by which business corporations are directed and controlled. The fundamental principle of corporate governance is to specify the objective of the institution, the client, and the product or the service that the institution provides, in order to enable the institution to be efficient and accountable.[5] State bodies tend to be highly bureaucratic and, because employment is secure, workers tend to be inefficient (Considine 1988). However, once a body is corporatised, it is required to take on more of the shape of private companies that compete in the market, and therefore—in theory—the corporatised body will act more efficiently.

Privatisation and corporatisation were first launched on a large scale after the second oil shock and worldwide economic downturn beginning in 1975. They gained momentum under Margaret Thatcher in the United Kingdom in 1979 and Ronald Reagan in the United States in 1981. Thatcher cut public expenditure sharply in a slew of privatisations, and elements of the market economy were introduced even into areas such as education and health care (Swinnerton-Dyer 1995). Similar measures were taken in United States, where there had been a rapid expansion in the student population, as well as in the number of higher education institutions (Kitamura 2001:137).[6] As the government no longer was able to support higher education institutions fully, the corporatisation of public universities seemed an ideal solution. Despite differences in historical backgrounds and socio-political environments, the corporatisation of public universities has been a common path pursued by industrialised societies such as the United Kingdom, United States, Germany, France and Japan.

These common changes are often explained as one example of isomorphism, or structural homogeneity, that is 'a constraining process that forces one unit in a population to resemble other units that face the same set of environmental conditions' (DiMaggio & Powell 1983:149). The key causes of university isomorphism are 'environmental pressure (especially government regulation) as well as dominance of academic norms and values (especially academic conservatism)' (van Vught 1997, cited in David 2002). Hannan and Freeman explain, 'isomorphism can result because nonoptimal forms are selected out of a population of organizations or because organizational decision makers learn appropriate responses and adjust their behaviour accordingly' (Hannan & Freeman 1977, cited in DiMaggio & Powell 1983). The intensifying competition among higher education institutions places them under pressure to innovate, but in a shared environment. Stensaker and Norgard (2001) describe this double-sided pressure 'to be innovative with a specific organisational mission while at the same time being an integrated part of a growing, and highly interconnected, internationalised and standardised higher education "industry"'.

## Malaysia's case

The reform of public universities in Malaysia has followed a similar course to that described in other countries. In Malaysia, the massification and democratisation of higher education has only just begun. With 22% of the age group of 17–22 in higher education, Malaysia is shifting from Trow's elite higher education to mass higher education. The government aims to achieve 40% participation by 2020. The Minister of Education, Tan Sri Musa Mohamad, stated in his speech at the MAPCU National Higher Education Conference in 2003 that Malaysia should prepare to move to a mass higher education system with the help of private higher education institutions. Growing pressure for the university to develop curriculums relevant to the world of work is also impacting on the development of Malaysia's universities. Several measures have been introduced to assess the quality of Malaysia's higher education institutions, as a means of ensuring accountability. These will be discussed in the next chapter. Furthermore, as we have noted briefly, the Malaysian government has moved to corporatise its public universities.

All these aspects suggest isomorphic changes shared with universities in industrialised countries. However, it is interesting to note that the factors propelling the direction of change in Malaysia's universities have often been different from those affecting universities in industrialised countries.

## Differences in general background

Unlike the developed countries, Malaysia still does not have enough higher education institutions to meet the public's needs, and both demand and supply of tertiary education are growing strongly. During the 2003/2004 academic session, a total of 37,034 places were offered, as compared to 32,752 places the previous year, an increase of 13% (Indramalar 2003).[7] Private higher education institutions have been increasing rapidly in number and they play an important role in democratising higher education. Nonetheless, as private institutions are still relatively young and their tuition is more expensive than in public institutions, for the most part students still prefer the public institutions over the private.[8] Consequently, entry to the public institutions is highly competitive. Student consumerism is not very strong yet, though it has more effect on the private institutions.

Malaysia's demographics also differ from those of developed countries. As of 2004, Malaysia enjoyed steady population growth of 1.83 % per annum (index mundi 2005)[9]. Figure 4 indicates that Malaysia's universities do not need to worry that a decreasing birth rate will affect future enrolments, as is the case in developed countries; rather, demand for higher education will continue to grow.

*Figure 4: Population composition*

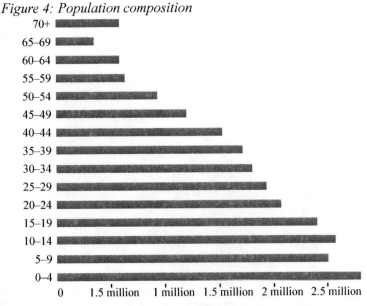

US Census Bureau, International Data Base 2006[10]

## Involuntary attendance

The phenomenon of involuntary attendance is evident in Malaysian public universities, but in Malaysia's case it is not due to a shift to mass higher education. On the contrary, as we have seen, competition for places is keen. In Malaysia's case, it results in part from the quota system. The ethnic quotas on entrance to particular faculties in public universities have often forced both Bumiputera and non-Bumiputera students to major in subjects that are not their first choices. Moreover, several senior academics at Malaysian universities indicated that students tend to choose faculties or their field of study depending on their scores in pre-university examination results, and that this leads to low levels of participation and motivation among students.

The establishment of private higher education institutions, as well as other alternative research institutions, has attracted academics away from public universities, for they have better salary schemes. For example, during 1996, the Medical Faculty at UKM lost two professors and 18 associate professors in six months, bringing the number of vacant lecturer posts at UKM to 90 (Lim 1997). Also in 1996, 25 lecturers quit UM. The 'brain drain' became an increasingly serious issue for public universities, and yet the government kept increasing the number of universities as well as enrolments for each university. As a consequence, public universities face a shortage of qualified teachers. In Malaysia, the competition is not for students but for academic staff. The results are interestingly similar to those of student consumerism, with pressure on the government to improve staff conditions, especially academic salaries, and a lack of staff involvement in research activities. The phenomenon of 'dead wood', academics who give up active research after achieving the rank of professor, is not, however, peculiar to Malaysia.

## Pressure from the world of work and relevance

Malaysian universities are certainly under pressure to deliver education that is relevant to the world of work or the needs of the market or the society. In the Malaysian case, this pressure most directly stems from concern in government and the wider society over rising numbers of unemployed graduates, leading the government to require public universities to re-examine their academic programs. Three issues concerning graduates and their ability to work are well known; namely, lack of English proficiency, lack of communication skills and an inability to work in teams.[11] It also appears that the unemployed graduates are mainly from Islamic studies and humanities disciplines.

Malaysia thus finds itself in a contradiction: on the one hand there are not enough universities, while on the other hand there are too many unemployed graduates. The disparity between university education and the requirements of industry is becoming a serious issue. In an effort to bridge the gap between the education sector and industry, ties are being developed between the two sectors. For example, UTM launched the University–Industry Technology Advancement Program in 1996, which was supported by Mahathir (*New Straits Times* 1996).

## Isomorphic change in Malaysia

Insofar as the conditions and problems affecting Malaysia's public universities differ in important aspects from those facing universities in industrialised countries, how can we account for the isomorphic changes that have occurred in Malaysia's public universities? For an explanation we must turn to the forces of globalisation as they impact directly on the higher education sector, and indirectly through the Malaysian government's adoption of the policy of privatisation of public facilities, again as a response to global competitive forces.

Globalisation is generally understood 'to be primarily a process of economic integration in which the owners of capital, financiers and money managers, among others, have been able to overcome the constraints of nation state boundaries to bring about global economic integration' (Gopinathan 1995:74). As Malaysia has an open economy and competes in international markets, economic globalisation has put pressure on Malaysia to be able to compete with other countries. At the same time, emergence of the knowledge economy has created a need to produce suitable knowledge workers (McMahon, 1992:465). For this reason, the Malaysian government espouses the aim of establishing world-class education, and public universities such as UM, USM and UKM emphasise internationalisation of the university as one of their goals.[12] The former Minister of Education, Tun Abdul Razak, speaking on the challenge of globalisation, asserted that the Malaysian education system has been undergoing a reformation in order to deliver world-class education (Razak 1997). Thus, competitive pressure leads individual countries, including Malaysia, to follow mainstream changes.

A further aid to understanding why isomorphic change is evident in Malaysia is the 'catch-up' industrialisation theory. Catch-up industrialisation is the pattern wherein late-starting industrialisers benefit from being able to adopt the technologies and practices of already-industrialised countries. Akira Suehiro has applied the catch-up theory to account for some of the characteristics of the evolution of higher education in developing countries (Suehiro 2000:chapter 12). As the catch-up approach has been adopted by the Malaysian government in other sectors, it provides a credible explanation for reforms in Malaysia's public universities that are modelled on overseas experience.

The pressures of globalisation and the catch-up mentality also underlie the Malaysian government's introduction of privatisation policies. As discussed in the previous chapter, the privatisation policy was launched by Prime Minister Mahathir in the early 1980s, a time when it was in sync with emerging global trends. The higher education sector was not immune from this trend, and privatisation came to it in two guises. First, the government relinquished its near monopoly control of the higher education sector, at first by default, but after 1995 as a matter of explicit policy. Second, again after 1995, the government commenced the process of corporatising the public universities. The implications of these changes will be the topic of the next chapter.

## Conclusion

The theories and models of change in universities derived from conditions in the industrialised countries offer some insights into the reform of Malaysia's public universities, though the Malaysian context clearly differs in important ways from that of the industrialised countries. The primary factors influencing the reform of Malaysia's public higher education in the 1990s have been globalisation and the privatisation policy. The measures themselves might be effective and innovative; however, as we have seen in earlier chapters, Malaysia's education policy has hitherto had to accommodate other national policies and social responsibilities. We are therefore justified in asking whether—or how—these latest reforms are working.

# Notes

1    John Henry Newman was involved with founding the new Catholic University of Ireland. He gave a series of lectures that culminated in *The idea of a university*, which is considered one of the most influential treatises on higher education in the Western tradition (Newman 1976:introduction).

2    For in-depth analysis, see Trow (1972).

3    Interview with Don Anderson, Professor Emeritus, Center for Continuing Studies, Australian National University, 22 May 2003. This concern is also seen among Japanese academics. Japanese public universities were corporatised in 2004 and there were heated discussions, as I learned during interviews I conducted in Japan in 2002, and also from articles in the major newspapers such as *Asahi Shinbun* and *Nihon Keizai Shinbun*.

4    This is true in the case of Japan, Malaysia and the Philippines.

5    Cited on the website www.encycogov.com. The OECD (1987) explains: 'The corporate governance structure specifies the distribution of rights and responsibilities among different participants in the corporation, such as, the board, managers, shareholders and other stakeholders, and spells out the rules and procedures for making decisions on corporate affairs. By doing this, it also provides the structure through which the company objectives are set, and the means of attaining those objectives and monitoring performance.'

6    Between 1960 and 1970, the number of students had grown from 3.6 million to 11 million and the number of institutions from 2008 to 3150 respectively.

7    Avaliable on the website www.studymalaysia.com.

8    There are some well-established private institutions, however, that public universities fear losing students to, such as Taylors College, Sunway College and HELP University College. Interview with Nina Adlan (editor, *Education Quarterly*, 22.10.2002).

9    Index mundi, http://www.indexmundi.com/g/g.aspx?c=my&v=24

10    http://census.gov/cgi-bin/ipc/idbagg

11    Institut Penyelidikan Pendidikan Tinggi Negara (National Higher Education Research Institute) USM has conducted a study on the unemployment issue in 2002 but the paper was yet to be published when I was in the field.

12    Internationalisation of the university means the exchange of students and staff internationally and meeting the international standards of research and education.

# chapter three

# Malaysia's public university reform

## Introduction

In Malaysia, corporatisation of public universities was not discussed in the early phase of the privatisation policy. As we have seen, the possibility was first publicly raised by the then Vice-Chancellor of UM, Abdullah Sanusi, in 1995 (Gomez, E 2003). Subsequently, with the amendment of the UUCA in 1995, the government laid the framework for corporatising all public universities. UM was corporatised on 1 January 1998, followed by UKM, USM, UPM, and UTM on 15 March 1998. Describing the institutions as 'bastions of conservatism and elitism', the Minister of Education, Tun Abdul Razak, said that universities needed to be made 'more responsive, more dynamic and more business-like' (*Asian Business* 1996). In order to make them more accountable and efficient, the structure of university governance was to be brought more in line with corporate management strategies. Concepts such as total quality management, benchmarking and mission statements were introduced. At the same time individual universities also began introducing certain quality management measures and aspects of corporate culture.

## Implementation of corporate management structure

According to Marginson and Considine (2000:7), university governance is:

concerned with the determination of value inside universities, their systems of decision-making and resource allocation, their mission and purposes, the patterns of authority and hierarchy, and the relationship of universities as institutions to the different academic worlds within and the worlds of government, business and community without. It embraces 'leadership,' 'management' and 'strategy'.

Traditionally, decision-making processes tended to take a long time in universities, especially on academic matters, which needed to be discussed in the Senate. In UM the Senate comprised over 200 members, including all professors, deans of faculties and heads of departments. This slowed the university's response to a fast-changing environment. It was argued that a corporate management structure and corporate style of good governance would improve the situation. The aim was to 'optimise and increase the effectiveness and efficiency in management of the university through the [better] utilisation of its physical and human resources' (Ali 2000). The new structure introduced under the amended UUCA aimed to speed decision-making and to make procedures more transparent.

Under the new system, the Vice-Chancellor has taken on the role of the chief executive officer and has been given greater power in the decision-making process. The council, which previously had 16 members, has been replaced with a board of directors of only eight members, including a chairman, the Vice-Chancellor, one representative from each of the Ministries of Finance and of Education, one to represent the community where the university is located, and at least three with experience or knowledge that might be of benefit for the board or from private sector (Universities and University Colleges Act:section 16). The Minister of Education appoints all board members, after consultation with the board in the case of the Vice-Chancellor. The board is the executive body of the university and is responsible for policy-making.

Membership of the Senate has been reduced from over 200 to about 40. It now comprises the dean of each faculty and professors elected or appointed by the Vice-Chancellor (Universities and University Colleges Act:section 16).[1] The Senate is the university's principal academic body, responsible for academic matters. With fewer people involved, it takes less time to discuss matters. However, anything decided at the Senate needs the Vice-Chancellor's approval and possibly ministerial approval. If, for example, the Senate decides to create a new course that requires new teaching staff, it needs approval from both the Minister of Education and the Minister of Human Resources.

The 'top university administration'—a term current at UM—comprises the deputy Vice-Chancellors, a registrar (also known as the general manager for administration), a bursar (also known as the financial controller) and a chief librarian. They are responsible for non-academic matters including property development, development of physical infrastructure and so on.

In order to promote corporatisation of the university, both UM and USM established a corporate development division to help the Vice-Chancellor and the Chancellery to formulate policies and long-term planning for the university. This division examines issues related to the corporatisation process, and organises seminars and promotes discussions. It carries out the self-evaluation of all internal operational procedures, and develops plans to promote better understanding of the corporatisation policy.

## Business of a university

Corporatisation gives the university the right to generate its own income. It is able to engage in market-related activities such as entering into business ventures, raising endowments, setting up companies, and acquiring and holding investments (Lee 2004:18). In principle it thus gains more institutional autonomy as, in general, institutional autonomy and financial independence are strongly related (Considine 1988). A funding body can influence administration by changing the amount or allocation of the budget. For example, if the government decides to focus on IT industries, it can allocate more money for IT-related education. The Malaysian government is certainly willing to use this influence. In such a relationship, the government controls or strongly influences the administration of the institution.

Financially, the public universities are still only partly corporatised. Because of the 1997 economic crisis, they were not immediately made financially independent, and there are limitations on their freedom of action. For instance, universities are not allowed to raise tuition fees at their discretion, particularly at the undergraduate level (Lee 2001b). However, the plan is that from 2010 they will be financially independent (though still partly funded by the government).

The universities have begun to embark on income-generating business activities. For example, some universities have begun to franchise their courses with local private colleges; distance learning and continuous learning courses have been provided; and individual academics are encouraged to engage in consultancy work with private industries, the government or other institutions. Both UM and USM have institutionalised their market-related activities. USM has set up a holding company, USAINS, which functions as its corporate arm, acting as the sole distributor and outlet of all commercial activities of USM and managing business activities such as the franchising of courses, consultancies, testing, contract research, rental of space and continuing/extension courses (Lee 2001b). UM also announced the setting up of a holding company in 2003 as a means of working towards financial independence in 2010 (*Star online* 2003a).

## Quality assurance

Another significant part of the reform is the introduction of various new quality management systems. A study by Anderson, Johnson and Milligan (2000) points out that 'quality' and 'quality assurance' are recent imports into the university vocabulary from industry and that academics are more used to talking about 'standards'. Both 'standard' and 'quality' are slippery concepts, especially in the university context. Quality can mean different things depending on 'whose quality' we are talking about and 'what quality' we are assessing.[2] The university has a multiplicity of functions and a variety of internal structures, but this complexity tends to be simplified in the corporate model. According to William Bostock, 'the corporate university has the predominating characteristics of being an institution that pursues technical excellence and…that follows a supplier/customer model of the basic educational relationship' (Bostock 1998:3). Not surprisingly, its quality management methods are strongly influenced by the supplier/customer model.

Public universities are now required to ensure that they have quality education for 'customers' and to prove that by making them 'marketable'.[3] Prior to 1996, there were several methods of quality assurance to ensure the quality of programs, teaching and research. Various bodies such as the National Higher Education Council, Ministry of Education Committee on Higher Education, Committee of Vice-Chancellors and the Committee of Deans, as well as various professional bodies, have been responsible for overseeing quality; however, according to Molly Lee, 'there was a felt need to establish a formal system and a central agency to be responsible for quality assurance in public universities' (Lee 2004).

Both UM and USM have formulated targets for enhanced quality. UM has brought up the idea of *Asas Pembentukan 5M* (5M quality program). The 5M includes *manusia berkualiti* (quality *m*an[power]), *pengurusan berkualiti* (quality *m*anagement), *pemasaran berkualiti* (quality *m*arketing), *kewangan berkualiti* (quality *m*oney) and *infrastruktur berkualiti* (quality *m*achine).[4] UM considers that improving these five elements of the university would lead the university to achieve total quality. How UM is going to improve these elements will depend on individual quality assurance programs. The approach taken by USM is different. It presents three strategic projects: the World-Class Competitiveness Program, the Healthy Campus Program and a project to improve the physical development of the campus. In order to offer world-class programs, USM launched the Nobel Prize Project, under which, by 2020, USM aims to deliver the first Malaysian Noble Prize winner (USM 2001).

These are rather general targets, but it is clear that both UM and USM are sensitive to the perception that they need to treat students as consumers, to the demand for better service from the society, and to the demand to meet international standards of teaching and researching. They are aware that they need accepted quality management measures to prove their quality to those outside the university. Thus, various quality assurance schemes and management techniques have been introduced, namely the MS ISO 9000 certificate[5], internal and external auditors, total quality management and performance indicators. Different quality assurance measures apply to different activities of the university.

## Quality assurance division

In December 2001, the government announced the setting up of the Quality Assurance Division (QAD) in the Department of Higher Education, Ministry of Education, to manage and supervise the quality assurance systems of the public universities (Lee 2004). Universities are now required to conduct a self-study of the institution and create an institutional database using guidelines set by QAD. The self-study is conducted by a team, with the dean as the chairperson and administrators, academics, students and alumni included as necessary. The self-study is required to make clear the strengths of the institution in meeting its objectives, areas of concern that need to be addressed, strategies for maintaining and enhancing the strengths, steps that have been taken to address the problem area and recommendations for change.[6] After submission of the self-study, the report is evaluated in QAD and a quality assurance assessment team is sent to the institution to conduct an audit. This team consists of academics and specialists who are well known in the field related to the program being assessed. The team uses *Quality assurance in public universities of Malaysia: code of practice* as a guide. QAD sets criteria and guidelines for good practice covering nine aspects of the structure and process of higher education, namely:

1. Vision, mission and objectives

2. Program design and teaching–learning methods

3. Student assessment

4. Student selection and support system

5. Academic staff

6. Educational resources

7. Program evaluation

8. Leadership and governance

9. Continuing improvement.

These aspects are rated after the audit and the result sent to the institution. QAD began sending audit teams to public universities in 2003.

## International Standards Organisation

The standards of the International Standards Organisation (ISO) were originally designed for the manufacturing sector and later extended to include service industries. A prefix to the standard indicates the country that is using the ISO, for example, MS ISO 9000 indicates a Malaysian standard.

In 1996, the government issued Development Administration Circular No. 2, titled *Guidelines for implementing MS ISO 9000 in the civil service*, in an effort to achieve the New Public Administration paradigm. It was announced that all government agencies must implement MS ISO 9000 by the year 2000 in order to ensure that the quality of service provided by the public sector was as good as, if not better than, that offered by the private sector. The National Institute of Public Administration was entrusted with the responsibility of providing the necessary training, while the Malaysian Administrative Modernisation and Management Planning Unit was given the responsibility of providing consultancy to prepare agencies to plan and implement the MS ISO 9000 series (Shafie & Manogran 1999:preface & chapter one).

At UM, university staff appointed as internal auditors undergo seminars and training organised by the National Institute of Public Administration. To maintain objectivity, the internal auditors are chosen from a variety of backgrounds, and after the training they are sent to a different section to conduct an audit according to the manuals. One feature of MS ISO 9000 is the record-keeping. Records provide the evidence that the quality system is being implemented. In order to acquire the MS ISO 9000 certificate, everything must be documented and the process must be transparent to prevent any type of corruption. Consequently, workers in a university, whether academic or administrative, also have to document what they have done. For academics, the documentation includes records of students' attendance, his/her own research proposals and plans, course outlines, reading lists and so on. At the same time, academic staff members now receive job descriptions, making the criteria for promotion clearer.

The universities, themselves, have also been developing indicators to check the quality of education and research. These indicators have been developed by studying United States and Australian indicators, as well as with the co-operation of the Association of South-East Asian Nations (ASEAN) universities network (academic, administration). Among members of the ASEAN universities network, Singapore, Thailand and the Philippines have well-established indicators (academic, education). Faculties and schools are also involved with the development of indicators (academic, administration). Examples of these internally-formulated indicators are student–staff ratios, the number of library books per student, the percentage of academic staff holding doctorates, the employment paths of graduates and so on. By quantifying some of the facts of the universities, those indicators make it possible to compare the environment of education in one university with others.

## Conclusion

Malaysia's public university reform aims to improve university education by making it more relevant to the market and society's needs. The measures taken in Malaysia's public universities are not unique to Malaysia, but are in vogue elsewhere. Taken by themselves, the measures themselves might promise to be effective and innovative; however, as we have seen in chapters one and two, Malaysia's education policy tends to be shaped by overriding national policies. Therefore, it is important to ask how the measures work in the Malaysian context.

## Notes

1   According to Molly Lee (interview, 18.11.2003), the size of the Senate differs from university to university because the size depends on how willing the Vice-Chancellor is to include people in discussion.

2   Those questions are asked by Molly Lee, Tan Ai Mei, Don Anderson, Richard Johnson and Bruce Milligan in their studies.

3   When I asked interviewees about these terms, the answer I usually got was that 'customers' meant students and 'marketable' graduates meant employable graduates.

4   www.um.edu.my/nadi_/asas.html.

5   UM aims to acquire MS ISO 9001:2000, while UKM and USM aim for MS ISO 9000.

6   This information is cited from http://www.kpm.netmyne.com/qad/procedures. html.

# chapter four

# Views of academics on public university reform

> When changes have occurred, the professoriate has had influence in shaping them even when they were initiated by forces external to the university...In these and other instances, the professoriate has been able to shape changes so that they reflected, at least in part, their image of the university. In many cases, academics have been able to circumvent or weaken changes that they did not favor (Altbach 1977:3).

It is the academic's work, which includes lecturing, research and social service, that creates the reputation, culture and identity of an institution. Bess observes that, 'Each department produces warrantably valid research through publications, which, in total, are intended to add to the reputation of the institution as a whole' (Bess 1988:59). Even with the current transformation of the university, academics (and particularly the senior teaching and research staff) remain at the heart of the university, having control over the curriculum and, in most universities, a key role in governance (Altbach 1977:2).

When Clark attempted to analyse the transformation from traditional to entrepreneurial university, he found that among the five elements contributing to a successful transition, 'the stimulated academic heartland'[1] was indispensable. He explains that if academic departments oppose or ignore would-be innovations, there will be little change in the life of the institution. For Clark, the heartland is where traditional academic values are most firmly rooted, and therefore the newer managerial points of view must be blended in at that level. 'Whether they [the traditional academic departments] accept or oppose a significant transformation is critical' to predicting the consequences of the reform (Clark 1998:7). In this context, it is important to point out that a unique quality of academic culture is that academics are inclined to give their first loyalty to their discipline and professional body, which often leaves them uninterested in university reform.

This chapter will illustrate how reforms to higher education have been interpreted and understood by Malaysia's academics, and how the country's public universities have reacted to the changes.

To ascertain the views of academia, I conducted interviews in Malaysia between October and December 2002, principally at UM and USM. These two institutions were chosen because they are the two oldest public universities in Malaysia. They were corporatised in 1998, and both are research universities; yet they differ in other respects because of their historical, geographical and social backgrounds. UM, being situated in Kuala Lumpur, and as the country's first university, has come under the influence of government policy, and yet it has also been able to maintain a measure of independence. UM is widely considered to be the state's flagship academic institution, and its prestigious status attracts the best students and scholars. UM fits Clark's description of those 'universities that serve as flagships or elite institutions in their own national or state systems of higher education'(Clark 1998:5). Thanks to this standing, it can to some degree 'ignore the lack of steering capacity longer than others and can continue to depend upon [its] outstanding reputation and political clout for guaranteed resources and competitive status' (Clark 1998:5). In short, UM has not needed to react quite so urgently to the pressure to reform. Conversely, USM, as the second oldest university and smaller in size, is said to have a more innovative attitude.[2] Due to its focus on science, USM also tends to be more directly influenced by the nation's economic and social demands, despite being located away from the capital in Penang.

Twenty-eight interviews were conducted with ten academics from UM (four in administrative positions), six from USM (one in an administrative position), one from UKM, five from private colleges (one former UM academic), four journalists (one former UM academic), two retired UM academics and one former UPM academic. Interviewees were selected from different faculties. The style of interview was open-ended and, if necessary, the same person was interviewed for a second time. The purpose of the interview was to discover academic reactions to the public university reforms of the 1990s. After asking each interviewee about his or her professional background, the following issues were raised with the aim of eliciting views on several major issues I had in mind. The questions were not necessarily asked directly and sometimes took different forms. The issues were:

1. Are you satisfied with your working environment?

2. Please describe the structural changes that have taken place at your institution.

3. How do you account for the university's corporatisation, and has this been of benefit or detriment to the institution?

4. What are some key issues that your university currently faces, and what do you suggest are some of the best ways of tackling these issues?

To protect confidentiality, most quotes are not attributed to the interviewee by name; however, some indication of the field of specialisation and position held is indicated if relevant. It is important to understand that there are three generations of staff in Malaysia's universities today: the first generation is the seniors (over 50 years of age), who were mostly educated overseas and speak English fluently (in many cases English is their commonly used daily language, alongside their mother tongue); the second generation comprises those in their 40s and who have been trained both in Malaysia and overseas; and the third generation comprises those in their 30s, who have gone through the national education system with Bahasa Malaysia as the medium of instruction. Judging from the interviews, this generational background usually affects their points of view on issues related to public universities. For example, performance indicators have been introduced as a part of quality assurance measurement. Academics in their 30s generally welcome this measurement because it gives them a target to achieve, while academics in their 50s are not well disposed to this measurement because they feel their professionalism is being questioned. Other factors that may influence an interviewee's ideas on public university reform are whether the person is Malay or non-Malay, and whether the person holds an administrative position or not.

Generally speaking, interviewees were very helpful and were willing to answer the questions. Some of them warned me in advance that the discussion might include sensitive issues, in which case they did not wish to be quoted. At the same time, it was observed that discussion of the quota system and language issue, which used to be taboo, had recently been placed on the table for discussion, probably due to the fact that Prime Minister Mahathir himself had begun to talk openly about those issues.[3]

The nature of the work that academics are engaged in is highly professional and personal, and, therefore, for example, it is difficult to change the way a person teaches or does research. It became clear from interview responses that corporatisation did not have much impact on the daily activities of individual academics. In fact, the interviewees, by and large, were not overly concerned with corporatisation. At the same time, however, academics are aware that public universities are facing certain issues and are required to take measures to meet them. Issues that academics seemed to be concerned about include quality management issues; issues related to social, political and economical pressures; the changing character of the university; and the character of students. According to interviewees, the best solution for meeting challenges is to have strong leadership: not the administrative leadership that corporatisation suggests but, rather, leadership with academic credentials.

The purpose of using these interviews is not to generalise the ideas of Malaysian academics. The reported opinions do not necessarily reflect the overall view of Malaysia's academic community. However, the comments do provide insights into what is happening in Malaysia's public universities.

The rest of this chapter is arranged around eight thematic topics, which emerged in the responses. The first two topics are concerned with corporatisation, which was seen as the major change in recent public university reform.

### Topic one: Different understandings of, and reactions to, corporatisation

Academics generally understand corporatisation to involve a change of terminology or a change in the style of management made to reflect the new role of the universities as business concerns. When asked how they understand the impetus to corporatise the universities, and who they felt was responsible for this, interviewees pointed to two major purposes behind the implementation of the corporatisation process. First, corporatisation is about establishing a structure to let universities generate their own incomes so that the government's financial burden is lessened and academics can get corporate pay. Second, it is about giving more institutional autonomy to the universities.

It seemed that the success of private higher education institutions had convinced the government of the desirability of corporatising public universities. A senior professor in political science noted that the government had already introduced privatisation policies prior to the corporatisation of public universities and:

> the government thought it was fantastic to see the successes of private higher education institutions because without the government using money, education was provided, students were happy with what they got, and some of [the private institutions] were even making profits out of the activities.

Understandings of corporatisation seemed to be different among academics involved in administration compared with those who were not.

#### *Academics not involved in administration*

> Corporatisation is just a name. It stopped after [the] 1997 Asian crisis (academic, Faculty of Economics and Administration).

Prior to its implementation, there were three concerns regarding corporatisation, which led to discussion among academics working outside administration. Those concerns were the salary scheme, academic freedom and entrepreneurial activity by the university. Originally, corporatised universities were expected to generate 30% of their incomes. In return, academics were promised a pay rise. At UM, a 17.5% pay rise was promised. 'Teachers welcomed the idea of corporatisation because they were getting a pay rise' (senior professor, social science). The 1997 Asia financial crisis halted this plan. It was then decided that public universities, even after corporatisation, would continue to be supported by the government and there would be no pay rise.

The need for the university to generate money caused discomfort among academics.

> Immediately after the introduction of the idea, we were asked, 'Is your faculty capable of bringing in money?' So I began to ask myself, 'Am I here to make money?' We are not businessmen and we have never been trained to be that way (senior professor).

> What happens to those studies which are not of commercial interest? How about student fees?...In order to generate income, first we have to raise the fees and second the research activities should be to service the industries (dean).

> Should there be anyone who is against corporatisation, that is because the person feels that corporatisation trades our quality for quantity...We should be more sensitive to the social needs or demands and we have to balance them with our individual [academic] activities (senior academic, education).

Academics were concerned that the emphasis would be put on profit-making rather than on purely academic activities. A senior academic in the Faculty of Education stated:

> If corporatisation is about bringing in professionalism, then I agree with the idea. And if corporatisation promises the development of independence, so to speak to chart our own future, then yes. But if corporatisation is about making money at the expense of quality and intellectuality, then I don't agree.

According to one senior professor, 'it did not come from the grassroots'. In the case of UM, it was understood that the then Vice-Chancellor, Abdullah Sanusi, strongly pushed the corporatisation project at UM. The fact that he came from Petronas[4], the state oil company, and not from an academic background, caused stronger resistance to the idea of corporatisation among academics.[5] One dean said, 'Sanusi was a corporate man. He was an administrator but was not an academic'. Another dean conceded that, 'He was good at developing physical infrastructure'. In an interview with the *New Straits Times* newspaper, Sanusi had emphasised that he had an academic background by saying, 'I have an academic background and have published books and journals on various topics. I was also a part-time lecturer for 10 years in the economics faculty...' (Shariff 1995). However, it emerged from my discussions with academics that they do not consider his defence to be acceptable.

According to the academics who were interviewed, their daily professional activities have not dramatically changed since the implementation of corporatisation.

> Compared with 20 years ago, we have to do more...paper work and the size of the class on average grew bigger, so there are differences [in working conditions]. But I can't tell if it is because of corporatisation or just the way it is. We have always been fighting to find funding for research and thinking about the quality of education and such (senior professor).

Observing the changes in the design of courses and curriculums, I asked one academic whether changes to courses and curriculums in the mid-1990s were the result of corporatisation, as it is one of the major criticisms of corporatisation that the design of courses is now very market-oriented. He answered, 'In the mid-1990s, our school decided to restructure the courses...But this had nothing to do with corporatisation' (academic, School of Social Science). Thus, it is difficult to pinpoint which changes have been brought about as a consequence of the corporatisation. Because their day-to-day activities have not been affected greatly, it is natural for academics to say, 'Corporatisation is not working. It was supposed to give us more independence so that we could have made our own money. And by getting higher salaries we could have attracted better teachers. What did happen was the increase of fees. But apart from that nothing has happened.' This sense that corporatisation has not had a significant impact has inevitably meant that the discussion of corporatisation among academics has subsided. Consequently, views on both the pros and cons of the implementation of corporatisation were not often aired during the interviews.

Proponents of corporatisation emphasised that it would provide a better administrative structure. A senior professor said, 'Without corporatisation, public universities are tied up with so many things...for example, in order to introduce a new course it can sometimes take a year to process. So when I think about that, corporatisation is good.' In fact, as outlined in chapter three, the changes in administrative structure after 1996 meant that some decentralisation has taken place, which has resulted in faster decision-making processes in some areas.

## Academics in administration

> You are dealing with people so if you want to see dramatic changes you have to kill people and have revolution (academic, corporate division).

For those in the administration or the corporate division, the corporatisation process is well under way and their main challenge is to change the culture and mindset of the university. 'Ninety-eight percent of corporatisation is about how to change the minds of university members' (academic, corporate division).

'It is important to prepare [academic and administrative] staffs to face what is coming as changes' (academic, corporate division).

For the time being, corporatised universities can secure income from the government; however, the government announced recently that it would reduce the budget for corporatised public universities by 20% by 2010 (Indramalar 2003).

> We surely know that the government can't support us 100% in the future. So we have to learn to generate our own income but at the same time, we have to learn how to save the money we gain from the government (academic, corporate division).

This is one of the reasons why the universities need to discuss the efficiency.

> It is like the parent–child relationship. The parents say, 'You can have your own freedom but we are not going to support you. You have to find your own income', and the child somehow has to learn to survive in the real world. You can't just do what you like to do and ask for money as well (academic, corporate division).

## Topic two: Corporatisation and academics

Academics who are not involved in administration or the corporate division deny the progress of corporatisation regardless of seemingly obvious changes in university administration structures. Discussing the university reforms in 1997, the then Minister of Education, Tun Abdul Razak, spoke of reforming two dimensions of the universities, the hardware and the software. The hardware signifies a university's physical infrastructure and administrative structure, while the software includes curriculum and academic or university culture (Razak 1997:229). With corporatisation, the clear initial reforms have involved hardware: reducing the membership of the Senate, and combining a more centralised top administration with decentralised faculty-based autonomy. However, due to lack of understanding and discussion, reform of the software has not been making progress. As a result, academics who are not involved in administration tend to be ignorant about the corporatisation process.

### Lack of information

> What part of [the] university needs to be improved? Is it the management or the administration? Is it the research or the teaching? (senior academic).

A lack of understanding of the reform process among academics indicates that the logic and reasons for corporatisation were perhaps ill-defined, if not miscommunicated. As tends to be the case with any reform in Malaysia, corporatisation was introduced without giving much time for public discussion. As a result, 'When the government decided to corporatise universities, not many people knew what it was all about. Everyone had his own version of what corporatisation was. Generally what people said about corporatisation was all about the policy change' (academic, corporate division).

The concept of the corporate university itself has never been clearly defined. Moreover, there are very few public documents or statements on the corporatisation of public universities. 'When the corporatisation idea was introduced, I had my own understanding, others had their own understanding and the government had their own understanding. That was how the situation became chaotic in 1995' (academic, corporate division).

A lack of information cramped discussion among academics, as well as among the public at large. A range of interest groups asked for more information. When corporatisation policies were first implemented in 1996, a student movement sprung up to oppose them. Student organisations were mainly concerned about an increase in tuition fees. The president of the National Union of Malaysian Muslim Students, Yusri Mohamad (1996), stated, 'At this stage we see an urgent need for this proposal to be clearly elucidated and presented, fully unveiled and unwrapped'. Opposition leader Lim Kit Siang argued that, 'The corporatisation plans and proposals should be made public so that academicians can give their views and input'.[6] Francis Loh Kok Wah also commented, 'Corporatisation of the universities raises many serious questions…It is [therefore] sad, even shameful, that the impending corporatisation process is still shrouded in secrecy' (Loh 1996). At the same time, academics understand well enough that, 'If the government says they are going to do something, that should be done and that will be done' (former academic, education). This implies that, even if they had been better informed of the corporatisation plan, academics would not have had much influence over the policy.

**Topic three: Quality assurance**

The quality issue is one of the biggest concerns for the government, academics and society alike. For example, Abdullah Sanusi, former Vice-Chancellor of UM, commented in an interview that, 'When I was offered the job [in 1994], the university was going downhill…I nearly cried when I saw the science faculty with its 34-year-old benches, and old beakers and funnels' (Shariff 1996). Politicians and journalists often describe the declining quality of public universities by pointing out how Malaysia's public universities are slipping down the ladder of the top 100 Asian universities in *Asiaweek* magazine's annual survey. For example, Opposition leader Lim Kit Siang made the point that, 'in the *Asiaweek's* 2000 ranking of Best Universities in the region, University of Malaya was ranked a lowly 47th position out of 77 universities, with Universiti Putra Malaysia in 52nd and Universiti Sains Malaysia in 57th position'. On top of that, for many, the issue of graduate unemployment has thrown doubt on the quality of education at public universities.

As the democratisation of university education proceeds, there is more sensitivity to consumers' interests. 'Productivity' and 'efficiency' are terms often used when talking about quality these days:

> teachers should be aware that they are taking time from students. If a class has 30 students and your lecture is one hour, you have to consider that you are taking 30 hours in total from students. Therefore you have to give a lecture that matches [the value of] that time. If students say that they learnt so much within your lecture then your lecture is successful. However, if they feel that they did not learn anything, then that is a problem (former academic, education).

In this context, the new quality assurance schemes have been introduced over the past five years. By using such quality management measures, the university intends to prove that, 'We are doing something to show that quality is there' (academic, corporate division) and to motivate academics and non-academic employees to work towards better quality. However, among interviewees, these innovations were often seen not to reflect academics' views and also not to address the situation that has led to the declining quality. 'The problem setting is right but the policy-making is somewhat going out of the way' (former academic). In rather the same way as with the implementation of the corporatisation policy, this academic attitude can be explained by pointing to insufficient discussion of quality assurance measures, coupled with the fact that academics tend to have a rather fixed idea of traditional and elitist university education, which cannot properly be evaluated by ISO or indicators, but only through academic peer review.

## *International Standards Organisation*

> If you ask me, ISO is a big joke. You can introduce ISO to improve administration and management but when it comes to the education system, no! (senior professor).

As explained in chapter three, the ISO 9000 series gives guidelines and models for quality assurance. Originally it was designed for the manufacturing sector and later its application was extended to include service industries. Therefore, 'ISO gives the impression that the university is a factory to produce human resources' (academic, internal auditor). This impression was shared by several interviewees, and may reflect a wider resistance among the academic community to the introduction of the ISO. The crucial issue in the implementation of ISO is whether it should be applied to academics' activities, as well as to administration.

Both UM and USM have introduced ISO. UM is attempting to implement MS ISO 9001 across the whole university, while USM has introduced MS ISO 9000 partially to cover functions such as the library, registrars' and administration offices, human resource development offices and the University Hospital. To check the quality, transparency and efficiency of the administration, 'ISO is good because, first, there is a system in place and there is a flowchart, so if the administrator does not meet the requirement we can pinpoint where it goes wrong' (dean). However, when it comes to academics' activities, implementing ISO is not so simple, due to the wide range of activities. 'It will be difficult to implement ISO for the whole university... We will have an academic auditor on a faculty basis and the service areas where they deal with the public will be assured with ISO' (academic, corporate division, USM). Two major arguments against the implementation of ISO are current among academics at UM. They assert that the quality assurance model requires academics to document everything they do, which has increased their workload, while the credibility of ISO in checking the quality of academics' activities is questionable.

The government guide to implementing ISO in the civil service explains that one of the reasons for resistance among employees is that, 'Change involves additional work: in the case of MS ISO 9000, the additional work involves documentation, training, filling in more forms and the like' (Shafie & Manogran 1999:ch 5). This is the case among academics. Academics are now required to record important activities such as the schedule for a course, reading materials, a research proposal, students' attendance, students academic scores and so on.

> Now we have to check, for example, the attendance of the students...The attendance ought not to be the issue here. This is a university and not a school. If we spend ten to 15 minutes to take the attendance, then it is [a] waste of time (senior academic).

Documenting the work that academics are engaged in is not an easy matter. 'It is very difficult to do when it comes to teaching. We have to plan what we teach and justify as well' (senior academic, education). However, teaching is a highly individual professional activity, therefore, 'We can always write an excellent plan on paper but that doesn't mean you teach that way' (senior academic).

> Given the fact that I have my professorship from the education studies and have been teaching methodology, I think teaching should be given flexibility. I mean, we write down the objectives but I don't believe that we have to follow that. How we teach should be given flexibility (senior academic, education).

At the same time, there was consensus among the interviewees that the ISO would allow the system to root out 'dead wood' within the academic community (those who do not put much effort into their own research after becoming professors or attaining a senior academic position). Thus, 'ISO is probably useful to ensure that there is minimum quality there' (senior academic, education).

Attitudes differ between senior academics and junior academics. Senior academics, by and large, opposed the implementation of the ISO, and said they did not see any benefits in it. They explained that, given their long experience as instructors and researchers, they feel they already have a well-developed sense of professionalism. Therefore, they feel that an ISO job description 'will not motivate academics' (senior academic). Young lecturers, however, supported the ISO because it would oblige them to be disciplined in terms of planning courses and research activities. 'I found it useful to organise my activities' (lecturer).

ISO is meant to prevent corruption in any form. Most interviewees considered that there is unfair decision-making in promoting or recruiting academics, which they considered to be a kind of corruption. In arguing that the ISO can do little to deal with this issue, an internal auditor at UM explained, 'It should not be difficult to justify any decision regarding promotion or recruitment, because these decisions should be based on an individual's academic achievements. Only other academics in the same field can judge if this person deserves the reward.' A senior academic in geography also argued that an external monitoring system such as the ISO is not a substitute for the seasoned expertise of the academic when it comes to promotions and recruitment. 'No-one is a better judge of another's work than the academics themselves', he argued (senior scademic, geography).

ISO 9000 is a quality system and not a product or service standard, therefore it is important to understand that ISO 9000 does not refer to the quality of a product or a service. 'ISO 9000 requires the organisation to discuss with its customers and set the quality standard of the product or the service that is required by the customer' (Shafie & Manogran 1999:8). For that reason, 'Once our university successfully obtains ISO, we can prove that our quality [of administration] is fairly good but our products [that is, graduates and research] can't be qualified in that way' (academic, internal auditor, UM). This limitation is not well understood among academics who are not directly concerned with ISO. As a result, sceptical views are heard, such as, 'How can ISO assure the quality of education and graduates?' (senior academic). Even people who are involved with MS ISO implementation were not able to explain clearly the difference between MS ISO 9000 and MS ISO 9001. This shows how much this concept remains alien to the universities and the extent to which academics are indifferent to ISO except for the documentation that they have to do.

It is the attitude of people that can improve the system. Twenty years ago we
never had ISO but our faculty was the best in Malaysia and even in Southeast
Asia. But look at it now, it is so behind! (senior academic, UM).

## Performance indicators

Another quality measurement that both UM and USM are using is
performance indicators. They give 'a rough idea of the quality of a university'
(former academic, education) by looking at the number of books in the library,
the number of doctorates among its academic staff, the teacher–student ratio and
so on. But it is a mechanical concept, and quantity does not necessarily prove
quality. For example, 'The number of publications can't show the quality of
research that the academic conducts' (former Vice-Chancellor). 'It is difficult
to answer the question of whether we can actually assure the quality by using
indicators. But I think it is possible if we want to' (senior academic, education).
This interviewee explains that if there is a shared commitment to the standards
of the university and professionalism, then performance indicators will not
become just a numbers game. 'An ideal situation is that everyone knows what
UM wants to achieve; then we can work toward [that] together' (senior academic,
education).

According to an administrator, the purpose of using performance indicators is
to provoke discussion among academics. 'By pointing out some of the activities
of the lecturer or the department, we are hoping that they will start to talk about
issues.' This interviewee thinks that because the nature of the work that academics
are engaged in is professional, it is difficult to make criticisms; however, by using
indicators, a third party can point out what the indicators suggest as strengths
and weaknesses. Then the faculty, the school or the academic needs at least to
justify that what they are doing is right or else should improve.

Neither MS ISO certification nor performance indicators actually *improve*
academic quality, nor do they indicate the causes of falling quality. In fact,
the definition of quality itself is not clear. For example, 'Does having quality
education mean following the course outline precisely? If graduates are all
employed, does it mean the faculty has good education?' (academic, private
college). As Molly Lee stated to the author, it is critical to know 'whose quality'
we are talking about.

## Topic four: Root causes of the academic quality downturn

In [the] '60s and '70s UM had [a] very good reputation. I would say outside
interference was one of the factors which led to the downfall of quality
(senior academic, social science).

The government's decision in 1970 to introduce Malay language as the medium of instruction led to the departure of foreign academics. At the same time, the ethnic quota for admissions was introduced as part of the NEP, which 'gave an opportunity for Bumiputera students like myself to study at the university' (former dean). However, this affirmative discrimination is credited with causing a lowering of quality because 'Certain places were kept for Bumiputera students, and to fill those places we didn't necessarily get the best students' (academic, economics and administration).

> For example, the university needs to have [a] certain number of Bumiputera students in the Faculty of Medicine, so those Bumiputera students who are not qualified sometimes can get a place. As a result, those students are not motivated and often can't catch up with other students so in the end they take longer…to complete the degree or drop out (journalist).

For non-Malays, the decision to study at public universities and what field they decide to major in depends mostly on their academic results. In order to enter public universities, students have to enrol in Form Six and sit for the matriculation certificate, STPM. Non-Malay students wanting to enter public universities have been required to do extremely well in STPM because of quota restrictions, and even after spending two years in completing Form Six, there is no guarantee that these students will secure a place in the public universities. In order to lessen the risk, and if they can manage the financial burden, those students can alternatively choose to do A-levels at private colleges in preparation for study overseas. 'There are so many uncertainties for 17-year-old students regarding their future' (lecturer, private institution). As a result of the higher entry requirements applying to non-Malay students, those who gain places in public universities tend to do better than their Malay counterparts. As Lim Kit Siang (1997) states, this is:

> illustrated by the 1999 data where only 96 Malays obtained First Class degrees in University of Malaya compared to 259 non-Bumiputera students while in Universiti Teknology Malaysia, only seven Malays received First Class degrees compared to 95 non-Bumiputera students. [These] must be regarded as Malaysian problems.

Since the ethnic quota was a national policy, the university had no alternative but to follow the policy and change the make-up of the university accordingly.

An ethnic quota was also applied for the recruitment and promotion of academics. The public sector was encouraged to employ Malays and to place a certain percentage of them in all levels of work. While affirmative measures to secure more places for Malays in tertiary education were taking place, the move to replace non-Malays with Malays in the upper reaches of the Ministry of Education and in individual schools was also under way, but not so publicly. The result was that Malays gradually gained more secure control over decisions within the education sector (Thomas 1983:163). Today, there is hardly a non-Malay dean of a faculty and no non-Malay Vice-Chancellor.

> Career-wise, there is nothing for non-Malay academics at public universities. For non-Malays there is a lot of politics. You know, it is very political. This is happening not only in Malaysia, but particularly in Malaysia. If you are non-Malay...you reach [a] particular level and then it will be very difficult to move on! (journalist).

As a result, many non-Malay academics left the public universities in the 1970s and 1980s. Of the first three deans of the Faculty of Education in UM, all of whom were Chinese and had Harvard University doctorates, none was still in Malaysia in 1980 (Thomas 1983:165). 'After three Chinese deans, until today there is no non-Bumiputera dean at the Faculty of Education' (former dean, Faculty of Education).

Academics, regardless of race, have become conscious of power relationships, which they see as a factor in the declining quality of education.

> People would say if I can be the dean, I can be a professor. So it is used as the way to get the professorship. So here even if you do not have great academic achievements, if you are a great administrator, you may get the professorship. So we have on one hand those professors with academic achievements and those with more of administrative achievement (non-Malay senior academic).

The problem is compounded because those without much academic achievement tend to feel insecure once they take the top position, and proceed to protect themselves by choosing people who support them politically. Such people cannot give good academic guidance to other academics because they are inexperienced. 'This, unfortunately, ruins academic culture. There is so much politics and it is sad. A lot of self-interests come into the picture' (non-Malay senior academic). Many academics acquire the attitudes of a bureaucrat by being uncritical and displaying blind loyalty to their heads (Lee 2002a:23). 'As long as you don't rock the boat, you are free to do anything' (senior academic). This development runs counter to the ideal that 'university is a place where people can express their own view. If there is only uniformity in our opinions, it is no longer a university' (senior academic).

A former academic offered the analysis that:

> The development of higher learning institutions in this country has been handicapped. Since the 1980s it became part of national economic policy, so it didn't develop fully higher learning institutions, which is more in line with the philosophy of national education.

According to Royal Professor Ungku Aziz, 'changes in the education system were basically political compromises and settlements in nature' (*Bernama* 2002).

A good example of direct political intervention is the case of Dr Chandra Muzaffar. He was the Director of UM's Centre of Civilisational Dialogue in 1999 when the university told him that his contract would not be renewed. The Centre of Civilisational Dialogue was founded in 1997 and Dr Chandra was deeply involved with the development of the centre from the beginning. It was such a sudden decision that Dr Chandra, himself, was not prepared for the news and his students at the centre were left with their essays and examination papers unmarked. Dr Chandra had criticised the Prime Minister's sacking of the then Deputy Prime Minister, Anwar Ibrahim, and it was understood on all sides that the university's decision was political. This incident has been treated as proof of the violation of academic freedom and of how far the university has become politicised (Muzaffar 1999; Netto 1999; Lim 1999).

On a broader plane, government interference continues. As demand for higher education grew, the government kept increasing the size of undergraduate intakes for the public universities. 'It became a numbers game' (social science, USM). For example, the number of students at UM grew from 18,234 in 1996 to 28,505 in 2000, which caused a shortage of qualified lecturers, facilities and so on. The former dean points out, 'There is no-one who can say, "No, my department already has enough students and if we increase more the quality will be sacrificed".' Faculties expanded very quickly and new universities were established. In this process of democratisation of education, the question of quality was neglected. 'When we have the fast expansion of universities, the quality is not good' (former academic).

Even after corporatisation, which was supposed to allow for greater institutional autonomy, the government's strong influence has not been weakened. 'When 99% of financial support comes from the government, how can you expect to have autonomy? The biggest shareholder has the biggest say and that is what's happening here' (former member of the Senate).[7] Recently, the government announced that it would focus on science and mathematics education. Influenced by this policy, the Faculty of Education at UM now aims to intake 60% of students from the science stream and 40% from the non-science stream. The government can influence university policy very strongly through 'the government's quality assurance measures and appointment of key personnel' (academic, education). 'The person appointed by the outside is not based on the tradition of consideration of academic merit and performance' (senior academic). As an example, this interviewee mentioned the former

Vice-Chancellor of UM, Abdullah Sanusi, who came from the government oil company Petronas. As this interviewee was not the only one who mentioned non-academic based appointments, it is possible to say, at least, that this is the perception of academics who are not involved in decision-making.

One incident illustrates the government's ongoing interference. When Johns Hopkins University's School of Advanced International Studies organised a conference on Malaysia in 2001, the Foreign Ministry telephoned a dozen Malaysian academics and politicians advising them not to accept invitations. This move by the Foreign Ministry was seen to be a result of the souring relations between Malaysia and the United States in the wake of the imprisonment of former Deputy Prime Minister Anwar Ibrahim in 1998. Eventually, all the invited Malaysian academics declined to attend the conference, with the sole exception of Jomo Kwame Sundaram of UM (*FEER* 2001).

## Responding to market forces

Academics reluctantly admit that the pressure from the market is growing and universities inevitably have to respond to it. Before approving a proposed new course, 'The Ministry will check with the industries and see if those graduates from this new course will be employable. If the response of the industries is positive then we can introduce the course' (dean). Molly Lee agrees that it is now the market that will determine which courses to teach, which research initiatives to fund, which student markets to serve and which enrolment policy to adopt (Lee 2002a:7).

Academics from different disciplines have reacted differently to this trend. For example, academics in the Faculty of Engineering think it necessary to follow the market trends to a certain extent, but the difficulty is that market trends change so quickly.

> They [industries] have to compete in the global market so the demand is great. Therefore they need people already equipped with skills, but what they have to understand is that the investment on hardware and software and their expectation for students is quite high. For example, within one and a half years we have to change the computer hardware because it becomes too slow compared with the one in the market... What we hope to do is to train our students very strongly in fundamental engineering so that when they go into the industry, they can learn the [applied] skills easily (dean, engineering).

'Industries in Malaysia are not willing to invest in research and development. Research and development in Malaysia is more to solve existing problems rather than inventing new technologies' (dean, engineering). Again, if the nature of the discipline involves acquiring practical skills, it is easier to adjust to market trends. However, 'It is very difficult to encourage students to do postgraduate [study] unless we give scholarships, and not many people are coming back to the university to teach because it is better pay to work in private industries' (dean, engineering).

The Faculty of Science faces a different issue. At UM, the Faculty of Science caters for the largest number of students. As the number keeps increasing, the faculty faces a lack of facilities and ever-larger classes. At the same time, because science study is fundamental and not so much applied study, the faculty is required to justify the importance of its program. In response to such pressures, the faculty has introduced a course on teaching science, in which students will learn how to teach science in primary or secondary schools, so that at least its graduates are qualified to be teachers.

The establishment of private institutions also has an impact on public university education:

> Unfortunately the existence of private institutions [does] not help public universities to be more mature as an academic institution. Private institutions in this country seems to think that education is business…It pulls the public universities in [the] wrong direction. In other countries there is a pure academic competition [between public and private institutions] but not in Malaysia (former academic).

There is growing competition between public universities and private institutions. 'Private industries prefer private institutions' graduates because they think the quality of education is better in private institutions and the students are trained in English' (academic, economics and administration). Interviewees in public universities usually have the perception that public universities are still better than private higher education institutions. Meanwhile, academics from private institutions are quick to defend their institutions' credibility. 'Who says public universities are better than private? It is the public university who thinks they are better but it might not be true' (lecturer, private college). 'Gradually private institutions are getting better. For example, Taylors College is doing an excellent job. It is true that we are beginning to lose urban students to the private sector' (senior academic, economics). However, this is not of much concern yet because, 'After all, public universities still have better facilities, reputation[s] and better academics. If you are to study chemistry, for example, no institution but the public university can afford to buy expensive facilities' (lecturer, private college). 'If you want to do research, you have to come to the public [universities]' (senior academic). After all, 'only the rich have options to choose between the private institution or the public university' (former academic, education).

Identifying the root cause of declining quality is complex and politically sensitive. According to interviewees, the best solution is to give more autonomy to the universities, which they think is not happening at the moment. We will return to this theme in topic eight.

## Topic five: Language and quality

'The changes of language of instruction affected quality of university education greatly' (former academic, education).

The medium of instruction at national educational institutions was changed to Bahasa Malaysia in the early 1970s. This led to the decline in quality according to many academics. Despite this policy, 'most academic textbooks are still written in English' (former dean), therefore proficiency in English is still required. Although 'students' English knowledge is assessed before being permitted to enter the university' (dean), many students, especially those from rural areas, 'where they have less opportunities to use English in daily life, experience language difficulty in university' (journalist). As a result, 'students spend more time translating their texts from English to Bahasa Malaysia than actually studying the subject' (academic, engineering).

Lack of materials in Bahasa Malaysia is critical in science subjects in particular. To the question of why the translation process has not been successful, the dean in a science-based faculty answered:

As for science and engineering, firstly you need the knowledge of the field before you can actually do the translation, otherwise you might get the context wrong. Secondly you have to have language skill. The only people who can do the translation might be scholars at university, but we do not want to do that job because it is time-consuming yet we don't get benefit out of it. We would rather spend that much time to do research. But, of course, having said that there are a few scholars who do the translation. But I prefer to leave it in English because I know when students start to work they have to read material in English.

The language issue is also critical among academics. A senior academic observed, 'Young academics would not come and discuss issues because they are not confident with English'. A young lecturer in his 30s said, 'I am the failure generation of language policy. I can't write and speak well in English.'

Because of the language, it is difficult to invite external academic auditors.

The best way to ensure that our education meets international level is to invite external academic auditors from either [the] United Kingdom or United States. We actually used to do that. But it is difficult when the medium of instruction is not English (senior professor, Faculty of Geography).

It is unfortunate that in a number of schools, curriculum as well as graduate examinations are no longer being evaluated by foreign specialists. The Nationalist sentiments and parochial ideals tend to have blinded many scholars and left several programs and examinations unchecked for international standards (Khattab 2002).

The government has again begun to put emphasis on English education in order to internationalise local universities. Today, universities are encouraged to teach 50% of courses in English. Most interviewees agreed that such a policy would benefit higher education, and they welcomed the government's decision. 'It is always the first one or two generations that have to suffer from those language policy changes' (lecturer, private college).

The position of Bahasa Malaysia as the lingua franca of Malaysia is still insecure despite the national language policy. This is a sensitive political issue, as can be seen from a paper Dr Zainal Abidin Abdul Wahid, Professor of History, presented at a conference jointly organised by the National Association of Islamic Students and the Linguistics Association of Malaysia. In his paper, he reacts to the impact of the education-related legislation of 1995 and 1996 on the medium of instruction and, with that, the economic standing of the Malay race and national culture. He asserts that, as the new Education Acts allow wider use of English in higher education institutions, the use of Bahasa Malaysia will be limited, and thus the economic value of the language will decline. 'If national leaders in high positions and a part of the Malaysian citizenry themselves make a fetish of English, then the masses will be led astray' (Zainal, no date).

## Topic six: Character of students and spoon-fed education

The three dominant criticisms of local university graduates regularly made by industry are the lack of proficiency in English, the lack of knowledge in information communication technology and the inability to work as team players (Lam 2003). According to industry, these problems are due to the spoon-fed and exam-oriented education that universities provide, which tends to prevent students from being innovative and independent. The general response of Malaysian industries towards local university graduates can be judged from the following comment: 'The person from a company told me that he would not employ local graduates because they can't think well, can't write properly, can't commit themselves with the work, and can't speak English (academic, science).' Other interviewees spoke of similar reasons for not employing local graduates. Academics also agree that the character of students is generally very passive, as shown for instance by the fact that 'it is very difficult to get students [to] speak out in class' (academic, arts). Academics regard this as one of the biggest challenges they face. However, the weaknesses can be attributed not only to the universities' educational ineffectiveness, but also to qualities of the whole education system in Malaysia and the cultural attitudes of students.

A major barrier to encouraging student participation is often class size. Classes other than tutorials are too big for a lecturer to manage. The size of the class varies depending on the course and whether it is undergraduate or postgraduate. The biggest undergraduate class size I heard of during the interviews was around 200 students and the smallest was around 40 students.[8]

> It depends on what I teach. If I am teaching fundamental studies such as basic theory, then I have to give a lecture. But if I am teaching something that requires students' participation, then I try to organise in-class discussion (academic, social science).

One associate professor said:

> Well, if you have [a] big proportion of students it is hard to remember who has talked and who hasn't, so I prefer small class[es] so that I can point out everyone. Students usually have their own idea but [are] just shy to speak out.

In order to promote interdisciplinary studies, faculties or schools allow students from other disciplines to take some of the courses. As a result, 'Some students do not even have the basic'knowledge of the subject, therefore it makes it difficult to run the class (dean, engineering).' Further, students are required to cover syllabuses that are too large. '[Not many students continue to do postgraduate study, so] we are trying to teach everything. That's why our course is four years. It is actually a pity that we have to do [it] this way' (dean, engineering). 'We should not give so much…to do [assignments and homework]. It is more important how students spend time and think about one issue than have them overwhelmed with new things to learn and end up memorising the facts' (senior academic, education).

Inevitably, a lecturer has to evaluate students by conducting formal examinations. Students become accustomed to an exam-oriented education during their primary and secondary education. In fact, the competition to enter local universities is so keen that students have no choice but to study hard to get good marks in the crucial exams. In this context, students learn to memorise important facts rather than think. The government also thinks this is a critical issue and recently the Minister of Education, Tan Sri Musa Mohamad, announced that the government is trying to move to a less exam-centred education system by introducing more school-based assessment. Further, as some academics point out, 'Maybe it is due to our culture. In our culture students are supposed to respect teachers, which means students do not usually go against teachers'. However, one journalist in his 30s recalled, 'When I was at university, there was always freedom of discussion in the class and outside the class among students and with academics'.

Lastly, there is the Malaysian version of Trow's 'involuntary attendance'. A professor in social science pointed out:

> I am not trying to justify my insufficient effort to be a good educationist, but often students decide courses depending on various conditions and not on the interests that they have. Our students are very easily influenced by the seniors. A lot of students decide to take [a] course by receiving advice and information from friends and seniors.

This means that students are not always highly motivated. 'Sometimes students just want to take as many easy subjects as possible just to finish the degree faster' (academic, social science). Another academic in economics said, 'Nowadays, everyone wants to have [a] degree'. In this situation, it is often hard to see students' motivation and commitment to a particular subject.

The students' socio-economic backgrounds have also changed. There are no published statistics to show the socio-economic background of students attending public universities, but according to academics' assumptions, public universities are getting increasing numbers of female students (JPM 2001:157) and, more significantly, students from rural areas. This has changed the atmosphere of the universities. A professor from the Faculty of Education said, 'Students from rural areas are very naive. They are not ready to expose themselves in competitive society.' Those students tend to be passive and quiet in a classroom.[9]

For the above reasons, education in Malaysian universities tends to be spoon-fed and exam-oriented. It should be noted again, however, that the situation differs from faculty to faculty. For example, students from the Faculty of Engineering at UM organise a summer camp with other universities' Faculties of Engineering to exchange knowledge and experiences. They also work on projects together. 'Students are quite active' (dean, Faculty of Engineering).

In 2002, a Thinking and Communication Skills course was introduced as a compulsory subject at UM. A similar course was introduced at USM. The motive for the introduction of such courses is the relatively high level of unemployment among graduates and the government's requirement that universities equip students with these fundamental thinking and communication skills. But, as in the case of other policies, academics were not consulted on the implementation of these courses.

> There was no consultation before the implementation of this subject. The university organised a seminar to explain to academics what's this all about and, actually, many academics did not like this idea. But our voices were

not heard. Only a study was conducted from [a general] educational point of view [not considering the practices of various faculties] (academic, Faculty of Engineering).

In order to encourage student participation, individual academics innovate with different methods. One professor in the Faculty of Education puts his reading materials and lecture notes on a website, and students are required to read them in advance.

> When I started to do that, my colleagues thought I was doing the wrong thing because they thought students would not turn up to the lecture if they were able to get the lecture notes on the web. It turned out, however, my students began to be more active in the class than before.

## Topic seven: Institutional autonomy and academic autonomy

According to Nik Aziz Nik Pa, dean of the Faculty of Education, autonomy pertains to personnel management and financial management. When it was decided to corporatise Malaysia's five public universities, it was agreed that they would be given the right to manage their finances more freely. In that sense, the universities were going to gain increasing institutional autonomy. However, in a corporatised university, gaining institutional autonomy does not mean that academics have more influence on the university's policy-making.

'Since it is an academic institution, it is fair to say that academics should have the greatest say. Where in the world, can you find an organisation that has no representatives from the major activity?' (senior academic). This statement was made to oppose the structural change reducing the size of the Senate in order to introduce corporate managerialism. 'Academic influence in university policy-making has declined' (dean). The dean added, 'In the top management, the chief of the library, the financial controller and the registrar sit there. Formerly those people worked for us but today they tell academics what to do. This is something academics do not like.' Also, 'the administration is run more in line with commercial corporate strategy. Thus, management of university has become rather centralised' (academic, social science). In general, academics are worried that the Senate, without many academic representatives, might be inclined to follow markets and corporate culture. According to a study done by Mohd Taib Osman, an emeritus professor of UM, after corporatisation and the reduction of the Senate membership, the Senate became, according to some staff members, a rubberstamp—it began to not represent the academic body, not only because of the reduction of its membership but, rather more, because of the manner in which its reduced membership was composed (Osman 2002:50).

To represent academics' interests, there is a nationally based academic association known as Academic Movement Malaysia and institutionally based associations such as the Academic and Administrative Staff Association in USM and the Academic Staff Association in UM. When *Aku Janji* (loyal pledge) was imposed on civil servants, the Academic Staff Association in UM objected to it on the grounds it might erode basic academic freedom of speech. But, on the whole, academics as a group of intellectuals do not exert much power and influence in the governance of their institutions or in the public sphere (Lee 2002a:11).

By bringing in different methods to ensure quality, the universities have begun to standardise the jobs of academics, which has led to more restrictions on academics' activities. For example:

> Recently it was decided that for some period of time we can't take any leave. Because the school wants the results to be out on time, we are not allowed to take any leave during that time. But to me this is silly. If I finish my marking earlier, I should be able to take leave. But the school thinks by doing this...there will be efficiency' (senior professor).

According to an academic in the corporate division, however, the picture is different. He explains that, under the new structure, faculties are given more autonomy in three areas: in academic matters (awarding degrees and planning research), in recruiting and promoting staff, and in evaluation. 'Before, everything had to be discussed at the Senate where all deans, professors, and heads of faculties attended; then the proposal was evaluated at the university council, then went to the Ministry of Education. So it took time.' He also points out that in the new structure, the Vice-Chancellor gains more power. Judging from his further comments, the people who gained autonomy may be the administrators rather than the grassroots academics.

The view that administrators are not doing a very good job seems to be widely held by Malaysian academics, and there is a poor relationship between faculty and administration. This is not a peculiarly Malaysian phenomenon, of course (Boyer, Altbach & Whitelaw 1994:chapter five). However, given the fact that the institutional autonomy of universities in Malaysia is relatively low, academics are worried that in the near future when universities are corporatised fully, academic freedom and academic autonomy might be further sacrificed.

### Topic eight: The importance of leadership

> I personally believe that the concept of corporatisation would not automatically bring about the efficiency and increase quality [in education and research]. Because, all in all, that comes back to the ability of the manager to make the most out of what we have (former member of the university council).

From the statements made by the interviewees, it is clear that academics are aware of the pressures on universities and the need for reform, but they do not generally think that corporatisation or implementing quality management schemes are the right solutions. However, they overwhelmingly agree that it is important to have the right kind of leadership in place. While corporatised universities have gained more centralised administrative decision-making mechanisms, academics believe that it is more important for the university to have strong academic leadership.

In a university, there are two important levels of leadership: the Vice-Chancellor and the academic heads, such as the dean of a faculty and or the head of a department. The Vice-Chancellor is the person who decides the overall policy of the university after consultation; the dean or the head of the faculty or department decides the structure and research objectives of that unit. A good leader cannot be just a good administrator, but must also be a respected academic.

Academics believe that, generally, the current high-level leadership does not live up to this ideal. Ideally, the Vice-Chancellor should speak out on the university's position; however, in reality, 'The Vice-Chancellor won't say, "No. We believe in the importance of philosophy, history, fine arts, pure science and mathematics, so we will not change the design of courses to [be] more market-related"' (former academic). Since corporatisation, the Vice-Chancellor has gained greater power in decision-making. The Vice-Chancellor now has discretion over the appointment of academics to the Senate, where they can voice their opinions.[10] Naturally, the Vice-Chancellor may tend to appoint those who share the Vice-Chancellor's positions. 'Nobody can disagree with the top's decision. That's why we need a good Vice-Chancellor' (dean).

The academic head is involved in the daily activities of academics in the faculty or department. 'An academic head is an authority and respected academician who knows the field. The dean has to be chosen because he or she is respected for scholarship' (senior academic). However, after corporatisation, the focus of faculty activities has shifted from teaching to service. There needs to be a balance between those service activities and pure academic activities.

> A good head should be able to decide to what extent we would get involved with money-making and to what extend we should be engaged in pure academic activities (former academic).

> There is so much research which is irrelevant to industry sector and private sector, but [can be justified by] talk about society, culture and enrich[ing] the country...That is why we must have strong initiative [from those] in the university who dare to say that this is still important (senior academic).

# Notes

1   The other four elements are a strengthened steering core, an expanded developmental periphery, a diversified funding base and an integrated entrepreneurial culture (Clark 1998:chapter one).

2   This is the general perception that interviewees share.

3   This idea was discussed with editors of *Education Quarterly*, a magazine with its focus on private higher education in Malaysia. Nina Adlan, one of the editors, said, 'Before if we asked a question related to quota system, academics would shut their mouth and never talk about it. But today everyone talks this issue openly!' (interview, 22.10.2002).

4   From April 1986 to March 1994, Abdullah Sanusi was Vice President, Human Resource Management, Sector Petronas. From April 1994 to March 1996, he was Vice-Chancellor, UM.

5   This view was shared by several interviewees.

6   Lim Kit Siang is the former parliamentary opposition leader, and is the national chairman of the Democratic Action Party. He is highly critical of the government's policies most of the time; however, as he has been continuously examining and commenting on issues related to education, especially on higher education, I have made use of some of his statements.

7   This idea is shared among academics in other countries. For example, Professor Alan Gilbert, then Vice-Chancellor of The University of Melbourne, pointed out that governments are just as likely as any other funding body to seek to influence universities. He said, 'The irony is that government paymasters are usually the most demanding of all sponsors when it comes to trying to call the tune in the academy' (Buckell 2003).

8   Class size is not, of course, a problem peculiar to Malaysia. One private university in Nagoya with which I am familiar has a lecture with more 1000 students (interview with a Japanese academic working at the private university in Nagoya, 8.9.2002).

9   Some rural Malay students turn to the Islamic movement, called the Dakwah movement, in order to find a feeling of belonging and togetherness.

10  This is based on Molly Lee's analysis regarding institutional autonomy (interview, 18.11.2002).

# chapter five

# Dilemmas of the public university

From the 1970s to the 1990s, Malaysia's education policies were strongly focused on integrating the public universities into the national development program. Following the legislative changes in the mid-1990s, the policy focus has broadened. Greater emphasis has been placed on the market-sensitivity of university education: in line with this, the government began the process of corporatisation of the public universities and, thus, the introduction of various quality management schemes. The new policies suggest that the state is loosening its tight control. At first sight, corporatisation appears to give the universities institutional autonomy in exchange for a cut in the government's budgetary contribution. However, in Malaysia's case, the new structure of the universities' administrations, the patterns of recruitment of staff and students, and the introduction of standardised quality assessment by the government suggest that the universities' autonomy has not increased greatly in the course of corporatisation.

We also need to observe the distinction between institutional autonomy and academic freedom.

> Institutional autonomy is a necessary but not a sufficient condition for academic freedom, which is the right of academic staff to decide what to teach, to determine their own research questions and methods, and to publish the results of that research (Anderson & Johnson 1998:section 3).[1]

It may be that academic freedom is best protected in an institution enjoying great autonomy. But this is not necessarily so. In other systems, academic freedom is guaranteed by a government organisation that, nevertheless, imposes a heavy set of institutional controls on higher education (Berdahl 1990:7). As we saw in the previous chapter, the Malaysian experience confirms that institutional changes alone do not transform the university, because individual academics, who play such a critical part in the university's activities, do not readily change their notions of what it is to be an academic. Moreover, academics lack interest in most organisational matters that are irrelevant to their immediate concerns and their self-interest in pursuing their distinctive career orientations (Bess 1988:14). Substantive reform needs sufficient dialogue and discussion between the government and universities, university administration and academics, and within the society, all of which is largely absent in Malaysia.

What, then, are the effects of the recent public university reform? Where are the Malaysian public universities heading? As in earlier chapters, we can draw on scholarly analyses based on global experiences to examine how far they illumine the Malaysian scene.

## Same reform, different direction

Motohisa Kaneko, Professor in Education at Tokyo University, introduced a grid to illustrate the degree of influence by external elements on the university's management model.[2] This allows us to plot different countries' higher education systems across two dimensions—the vertical axis shows the degree of financial independence and the horizontal axis represents the degree of institutional autonomy.

*Figure 5: Influence of external elements on university management*

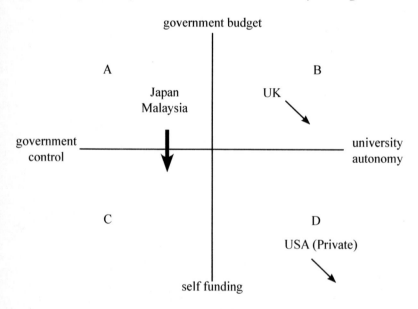

Universities in category A follow the state facility model. Universities in this category are created by the state and almost completely financed by it. In the 'state control model', to use Neave and van Vught's label, or the 'continental model', to use Clark's label, the state is most often the overarching and highly powerful regulator of the system (Neave & van Vught 1994:9–11). A national ministry of education regulates the access conditions, the curriculum, the degree requirements, the examination systems, the appointment and enumeration of academic staff, and so forth. Malaysia's public universities before 1996 fall into this category. Universities in category B follow the quasi-market model. This model includes universities that are largely funded by government but have relatively high institutional autonomy. The internal budget allocation remains in the hands of the university and the university is responsible for its own management. The traditional British universities, which Neave and van Vught call 'chartered corporations', are in this category.[3] Category C is yet to be named. Universities in this category have to be independent financially; however, the government somehow keeps strong control over them. Category D is the fully-fledged corporate model. The American universities belong to this category. Universities in this category need to generate their own incomes, as the government gives minimal financial support. In these circumstances there is very limited government control and regulation, but the influence of the institutional trustees and administrators is strong.

The importance of Kaneko's diagram is that it makes it clear how, even if the same process of corporatisation takes place, depending on other elements in the national environment, the reform could push universities in different directions.

Malaysia's public universities today are moving from category A to C.[4] The public universities are expected to make their own decisions and policies to deliver better service and to generate their own income; however, the government will not allow universities much institutional autonomy.[5] The dilemmas faced in public university reform in Malaysia stem from the awkwardness of this transition. Judging from the study by Neave and van Vught, universities in other rapidly developing countries also seem to be following this path of transition. There is a need for further observation and analysis to understand the processes, the relations between the state and the university, and emerging characters of those universities moving into category C.

## The power balance between the government and the public universities

There is an inherent tension in power relations between the government and public universities in all countries (Kitamura 2001:chapter five). As a national institution, the public university must be accountable to society and has a duty to comply with overriding national policies. At the same time, as an independent academic institution, it should detach itself from the society sufficiently to protect academic freedom and its institutional autonomy. In Malaysia's case, the government's power is overwhelmingly strong. This is because no individual university has had the opportunity to develop its own firm institutional culture and identity. All public universities in Malaysia have very short histories compared with universities in Europe, the United Kingdom and the United States. Except UM, all Malaysia's public universities were planned and established by the government with the express intention of meeting the objectives of national development policies. Furthermore, since Malaya's independence in 1957, the government has overhauled the UUCA three times, each time with major amendments. The frequent changes in education-related policies and legislation have not allowed the success of the changing policies to be evaluated. The public universities have been largely powerless in the face of these legislative changes.

Neave and van Vught see this as characteristic of universities in what they class as the Asian group (Neave & van Vught 1994). They use three groups—the Anglo–American group, the European group and the Asian group—based on historical differences in the development of university systems.[6] According to them, the Anglo–American group includes countries that, during the 19th and early 20th centuries, developed a strong tradition of distancing universities from intervention by the state. The European group includes countries where universities were established under legislation, giving governments considerable potential authority with respect to university administration. The Asian group includes countries where economic development is historically more recent, and where governments have tended to regard universities fairly explicitly as instruments for advancing national cohesion and economic advancement (Anderson, Johnson & Milligan 2000:14). The implication of this classification is that university systems in the Asian group will find it hardest to achieve a degree of autonomy from the government. This is certainly true in the case of Malaysia.

With the emergence of the knowledge-based economy, competition from private higher education institutions, the rise of student consumerism and the influence of the globalised economy, there is the growing need for universities to be able to react to various and sometimes conflicting demands more independently and in ways that preserve their institutional integrity. Rothblatt states, 'I would argue on historical grounds that universities can only be as flexible, as responsive, as progressive, as enlightened, as vital as the broader political traditions of their societies allow' (Rothblatt 1995:25). Reflecting on Malaysia's case in this light, we can see that the public universities are caught in the midst of divergent expectations and pressures in an environment where social and political issues, especially the ethnic and national language issues, make it difficult to change the balance of power between government and university.

## Race and national language

As a developing country with multi-ethnic society, nation-building with ethnic harmony has been a huge challenge to the Malaysian government, to which it has given high priority. 'Ethnicity has been too defining an element of Malaysian life and there has been no issue more emotive and divisive' (*New Straits Times* 2003). The challenge for the public universities is how to preserve academic standards and academic freedom within the constraints of national ethnic and language policies. Most interviewees agreed that the introduction of English and recruitment of students and academic staff based on academic merit would improve the universities' academic standards. It is only recently that, facing competition for skilled human resources in the global economy, the government has moved in these directions by re-introducing English as a medium of instruction in the public universities and removing direct ethnic quotas on the intake of students. Malaysia's open, internationalised economy has thus compelled a liberalisation of Malaysia's ethnic and language policies.

However, a change of government policy does not wholly resolve those issues because, in Rochblatt's words:

universities are indeed decisively influenced by the societies of which they are a part, only I would broaden the conception of society to take into account the contradictions, the variations, the complexities that do and must characterise any society that we can ever know (Rothblatt 1995:25).

In Malaysia's case, keeping an ethnic balance among staff and students, and promoting usage of the national language are two social responsibilities that public universities cannot ignore. Keeping the balance between English, the essential language for economic development and international scholarship, and Malay, the national language whose technical vocabulary remains limited, will be a great challenge.

## The public university as the guardian of fundamental studies

Another dilemma that public universities in Malaysia faces is the degree to which they should protect fundamental studies that enrich the nation's academic culture, but which might not bring money into the universities. 'How many private institutions have fundamental studies such as mathematics, chemistry, philosophy, literature, history, etc?...They are not trendy, they are not fashionable, and they are not marketable so none of the new universities can afford...those departments.' (former academic, mathematics) The private higher education institutions are relatively new and financially smaller than the public universities. They cannot afford, for example, to buy laboratory equipment for the study of chemistry, or to acquire books and journals for their libraries, but these are necessary investments for producing quality research outcomes and for the accumulation of intellectual knowledge. The public universities can afford this investment because they get support from the government budget. 'Making the society mature through teaching those [fundamental] subjects is the role of public universities' (former academic, mathematics).

At the same time, the public universities are pressured to be more relevant to the market and society's needs, and the further cutting of government contributions in 2010 will intensify this pressure. One of the effects of the expansion of market-oriented education can be observed in the increasing subdivisions in faculties and departments offering specialised courses that purport to equip their graduates with marketable skills. 'Universities are starting to have all those strange degrees [with very specific names such as maths and education, IT and management, development studies and management], which basically have no philosophy in its academic activities' (former academic). Thus, Malaysian public universities confront the problem identified by Trow: 'The growing popularity of specialised and vocational subjects among undergraduates has led to a concern in many colleges and universities for the survival of liberal or general education' (Trow 1972:189). Stensaker and Norgard (2001:473) concur:

> universities are increasingly facing a double-sided pressure: to be innovative with a specific organisational mission while at the same time being an integrated part of a growing, and highly interconnected, internationalised and standardised higher education 'industry'.

## The Leaning Tower of Pisa?

These are the dilemmas facing Malaysia's public universities. The perception of those who work in the universities and who observe them from outside is that, somehow, the image of the public university in Malaysia has shifted from that of an ivory tower to that of a Leaning Tower of Pisa. Everyone can see that something has to be done to rebalance the tower but no-one knows how. The tower retains a fading classical beauty—it could do with some refurbishment—but unless its foundations are strengthened, it will one day collapse.

The question is how this elusive balance can be achieved. Perhaps the new policies recently introduced are not all wrong. It is, rather, that there is the urgent need for discussion within the university community on how they should be implemented. The public universities seem to have reached a turning point and the time has come for academics to contribute actively to discussion of the future of their own national higher education institutions. Interviewees suggested that having strong academic leadership is the best way to survive this turmoil. If so, it is time for each academic and member of the administration to consider the present situation and to take their fate in their own hands.

# Notes

1    Autonomy has to be distinguished from academic freedom (sometimes called 'individual autonomy'). The academic freedom of an individual scholar is his or her freedom to pursue truth in teaching and research activities wherever it seems to lead, without fear of punishment or termination of employment for having offended some political, religious or social orthodoxy (Ashby 1966).

2    This model was introduced by Motohisa Kaneko at the Conference on Asian Higher Education held at Nagoya University, Japan, 18.12.2002.

3    During last two decades, British higher education is moving more towards category C.

4    This was pointed out by Molly Lee after Kaneko's conference presentation.

5    This is also observed in other countries. Marginson and Consideine (2000:175) point to this as one of the paradoxes of the enterprise university, saying, 'Universities are still shaped by the state, yet their individuality is highlighted...'.

6    This classification by Neave and van Vught is accepted widely and used, for example, by the Commonwealth (of Nations) Higher Education Management Service and the Centre for Continuing Education at the Australian National University when conducting comparative studies.

# Different forms of higher education programs

## Split degree programs

Arrangements with foreign universities allow partial completion of degree programs in local private higher educational institutions, with the final part of the programs completed at the foreign universities. The programs that fall into this category include the foreign twinning programs and credit transfer/advanced standing.

### Foreign twinning programs

These programs were established in Malaysia in the mid to late 1980s (Higashikawa 1996:123). They allow students to complete one or two years before proceeding to the twinning partner institution overseas to complete the degree.

### Credit transfer/advanced standing

Students complete part of their studies in Malaysia and the remainder at campuses overseas. This program is different from the twinning program in that colleges follow their own curriculums and students are able to choose which foreign universities they wish to attend in order to complete their degree programs. This arrangement was at first primarily geared towards education under the American Degree Program.

## Entire degree programs

The following programs enable students to complete degree programs as external students in Malaysia.

### '3+0' programs

The 3+0 programs allow Malaysian private colleges to examine, evaluate and run degree programs with the guidance of a partner foreign university. There are currently 35 colleges approved to run 3+0 programs by the Ministry of Education. They are under the scrutiny of the National Accreditation Board to ensure standards.

## Foreign external programs

Under these programs, Malaysian private colleges offer tutorials and administrative support to students while they are registered as external students of a foreign university. The foreign university decides the curriculum and entry requirements, and conducts examinations to its own standards.

## Open/virtual learning

This is the 21st century version of distance learning offered by the Open University and owned by the METEOR consortium of public universities. It uses a comprehensive package of study materials and CD ROMs, interaction through video conferencing, and email and Intranet systems, and is supplemented by some 'real' contact with lecturers and peers.

## Local university franchise programs

Certain local universities such as UPM and USM franchise their course guides and programs to local colleges. Those who complete the course work at private colleges are awarded degrees from the university.

# A chronological table of education-related events in Malaysia, 1956–2002

| Date | Higher education | Minister of Education | Selected political events |
|---|---|---|---|
| 1956 | | | Report of the Education Committee (The Razak Report) |
| 1957 | The University of Malaya (UM) establishes a campus in Kuala Lumpur | YB Dato' Abdul Razak bin Dato' Hussein | Independence of the Federation of Malaya |
| | | YB Mohd Khir Johari (1957–60) | Education Ordinance 1957 |
| 1960 | | YB En Abdul Rahamn Talib (1960–62) | Education Review Committee Report (The Rahman Talib Report) |
| 1961 | | | The Education Act |
| 1962 | UM becomes a separate and autonomous university | YB Kapten Hj Abdul Hamid Khan bin Hj Sakhawat Ali Khan 1962–64 | Higher education Planning Committee |
| 1965 | | YB En Abdul Rahman Talib (1964–65) | First Malaysia Plan |
| | | | MARA, Majlis Amanah Rakyat, Council for Indigenous Peoples |
| 1967 | Intitut Teknologi MARA established (becoming Universiti Teknologi MARA in 1999) | YB En Mohd Khir Johari (1965–69) | The National Language Act |

| Year | Universities | Minister | National events |
|---|---|---|---|
| 1969 | Kolej Tunku Abdul Rahman (24 February) University Sains Malaysia (June) | YB En Datuk Hj Abdul Rahman Yakub (1969–70) | Riots on 13 May The National Operations Council (Tun Razak) |
| 1970 | Universiti Kebangsaan Malaysia (18 May) | YB Datuk Hussein bin Onn (1970–73) | |
| 1971 | Universiti Pertanian Malaysia (4 October), becoming Universiti Putra Malaysia in 1977 | | Amendment of the Constitution Universities and University Colleges Act 1971 |
| | | YB En Mohammad Yaacob (1973–74) | |
| 1975 | Universiti Teknologi Malaysia (1 April) | YB Dr Mahathir bin Mohamad (1974–78) | Committee under the chairmanship of Dr Abdul Majid bin Ismail Amendment to the Universities and University Collegs Act |
| Late 1970s –1980s | Increase in the number of students going overseas | YB Dato; Musa Hitam (1978–81) | |
| 1980 | | | The Heavy Industry Corporation of Malaysia |
| 1981 | | YB Datuk Amar Dr Sulaiman bin Hj Daud (1981–84) | Mahathir becomes Prime Minister Look East policy |
| 1983 | Universiti Islam Antarabangsa (10 May) All courses at universities now taught in Bahasa Malaysia | | Privatisation policy Malaysia Incorporated |
| 1984 | Universiti Utara Malaysia (16 February) | | |

| Year | Event/activity | Minister of Education | Guidelines/policy |
|---|---|---|---|
| 1985 | | | Guidelines on privatisation |
| mid-1980s | Twinning programs | YB Datuk Abdullah bin Hj Ahmad Badawi (1984–86) | |
| Late 1980s –90s | Private higher education institutions becoming more numerous | YB Saudara Anwar Ibrahim (1986–91) | |
| 1989 | National Academic Conference at USM (October) | | |
| 1990 | | | The National Development Plan (July) |
| 1991 | | | Malaysia Privatisation Master Plan (8 Febraury) |
| | | | Vision 2020 (28 February) |
| 1992 | Universiti Malaysia Sarawak (24 December) | YB Datuk Amar Dr Sulaiman bin Hj Daud (1991–95) | |
| 1994 | Universiti Malaysia Sabah (24 November) | | |
| 1995 | VCs meet with Minister of Education to discuss a paper prepared by the VC of UM on the proposed corporatisation of UM and University Hospital (January) | YB Dato' Seri Mohd Najib bin Tun Abdul Razak (1995–99) | Restructure of Ministry of Education |
| | Corporatisation plan submitted to EPU and the workshop on corporatisation of universities is held at UM (May) | | |
| | Student demonstration against corporatisation of public universities | | |

| | | |
|---|---|---|
| 1996 | *Universiti Telekom/MultiMedi University*<br>Basic undergraduate program in all public universities shortened from four to three years | Education Act (amendment) 1996<br>Universities and University Colleges Act (amendment) 1996<br>Private Higher Education Institutions Act 1996<br>National Council on Higher Education Act 1996<br>National Accreditation Board Act 1996<br>Multimedia Super Corridor |
| 1997 | UM adopts new constitution<br>*Universiti Tenaga Nasional*<br>*Universiti Tun Abdul Razak*<br>*Universiti Teknologi Petronas* | National Higher Education Fund Board Act 1997<br>Asian Financial Crisis |
| 1998 | All other public universities adopt a new constitution<br>UM corporatised (1 January)<br>Kolej Universiti Islam Malaysia (13 March)<br>UKM, USM, UPM and UTM corporatised (15 March)<br>3+0 program starts<br>Number of overseas studetns from neighbouring countries increases<br>*Monash University Malaysia | Malaysian University English Test |

| Year | Institutions | | |
|---|---|---|---|
| 1999 | Kolej Universiti Sains dan Teknologi Malaysia<br>Kolej Universiti Terengganu (15 July)<br>*Curtin University of Technology, Sarawak<br>International Medical University<br>University Industri Selangor* | YB Tan Sri Dato' Seri Musa bin Mohammad (1999–2004) | Matriculation Division in the Ministry of Education |
| 2000 | *University of Nottingham in Malaysia<br>*FTMS-DeMonfort University<br>The concept of community colleges was raised in the budget discussion in parliament | | National Higher Education Fund Board Act (amendment) 2000 |
| 2001 | Kolej Universiti Teknikal Kebangsaan Malaysia<br>Kolej Universiti Teknologi Tun Hussein Onn<br>Open University of Malaysia* | | |
| 2002 | Malaysia University of Science and Technology<br>Universiti Tunku Abdul Rahman<br>*Swinburne Sarawak University of Technology* | | Legislation passed for teaching mathematics and science in English |

Italics indicate the name of a private higher education institution.
* indicates branch of a foreign university.

## Acronyms

| | |
|---|---|
| EPU | Economic Planning Unit |
| GIPTSB | Gabungan Institusi Pendidikan Tinggi Swasta Bumiputra (Union of Malay Private Higher Education Institutions) |
| ISO | International Standards Organization |
| JPTA | Jabatan Pendidikan Tinggi Kementerian Pendidikan Malaysia |
| MAPCU | Malaysian Association of Private Colleges and Universities |
| MARA | Majlis Amanat Rakyat Malaysia (Trust Council for Indigenous Peoples) |
| MS ISO | Malaysian Standard, variant of ISO. |
| MSC | Multimedia Super Corridor |
| NAPIEI | National Association of Private and Independent Educational Institutions |
| NDP | National Development Plan |
| NEP | New Economic Policy |
| NOC | National Operations Council |
| NVP | National Vision Policy |
| OECD | Organization for Economic and Cooperation and Development |
| OPP3 | Third Outline Perspective Plan |
| STPM | Sijil Tinggi Persekolahan Malaysia |

UIAM    Universiti Islam Antarabangsa Malaysia (International Islamic University of Malaysia)

UKM    Universiti Kebangsaan Malaysia (Malaysian National University)

UM    Universiti Malaya (University of Malaya)

UPM    Universiti Pertanian Malaysia (Malaysian Agricultural University), later Universiti Putera Malaysia

USM    Universiti Sains Malaysia (Malaysian Science University)

UTiM    Universiti Teknologi MARA (MARA University of Technology)

UTM    Universiti Teknologi Malaysia (Malaysian University of Technology)

UUCA    Universities and University Colleges Act

## List of Public Universities in Malaysia

Universiti Islam Antarabangsa Malaysia

Universiti Kebangsaan Malaysia

Universiti Malaya

Universiti Malaysia Sabah

Universiti Malaysia Sarawak

Universiti Pendidikan Sultan Idris

Universiti Putra Malaysia

Universiti Sains Malaysia

Universiti Teknologi Malaysia

Universiti Teknologi MARA

Universiti Tunku Andul Rahman

Universiti Utara Malaysia

Kolej Universiti Islam Malaysia

Kolej Universiti Kejuruteraan dan Teknologi Malaysia

Kolej Universiti Kejuruteraan Utara Malaysia

Kolej Universiti Sains dan Teknologi Malaysia

Kolej Universiti Teknikal Kebangsaan Malaysia

Kolej Universiti Teknologi Tun Hussein Onn

Adlan, Nina and Mark Disney 2000, editors, Education Quarterly, interview with author, 26 September.

—— 2002, interview with author, 17 October.

Ali, Anuwar 2000, 'Managing change in higher education', paper presented at the 5th National Civil Service Conference, Intan, Bukit Kiara, 22 June

Altbach, Philip G 1977, *Comparative perspectives on the academic profession*, Praeger, New York and London.

Andaya, BW and LY Andaya 1982, *A history of Malaysia*, Macmillan, London.

Anderson, Don 2003, Professor Emeritus, Centre for Continuing Studies, Australian National University, interview with author, 22 May.

Anderson, Don and Richard Johnson 1998, *University autonomy in twenty countries*, Department of Employment, Education, Training and Youth Affairs, Canberra.

Anderson, Don, Richard Johnson and Bruce Milligan 2000, *Quality assurance and accreditation in Australian higher education: an assessment of Australian and international practice*, Ausinfo, Canberra.

Anderssen, Curtis A 1993, *Educational refugees: Malaysian students in Australia*, Monash Asia Institute, Clayton.

Aronowitz, S 2000, The knowledge factory: dismantling the corporate university and creating true higher learning, Beacon Press, Boston.

Ashby, E 1966, *Universities, British, Indian, African*, Harvard University Press, Cambridge.

*Asian Business* 1996, 'Revolution in education', May.

*Asiaweek* 1996, 'Malaysia: in pursuit of excellence: Najib tackled politically sensitive reforms', 15 July.

Awang Had Saleh 1994, 'Phases of development of modern education in Malaysia' in *Malaysian Development Experience*, National Institute of Public Administration, Kuala Lumpur.

Berdahl, R 1990, 'Academic freedom, autonomy and accountability in British universities', *Studies in Higher Education* 15(2)

Bess, James L 1988, *Collegiality and bureaucracy in the modern university: the influence of information and power on decision-making structures*, Teachers College Press, New York.

Bostock, William W 1998, 'The global corporatisation of universities: causes and consequences,' *AntePodium, An antipodean electronic journal of world affairs*, School of Political Science and International Relations, Victoria University of Wellington, www2.vuw.ac.nz/atp/articles/bostock.html.

Boyer, Ernest L, Philip G Altbach and Mary Jean Whitelaw 1994, *The academic profession: an international perspective*, The Carnegie Foundation for the Advancement of Teaching, Princeton.

Buckell, Jim 2003, 'Unis face political pressure, V-C says', *The Australian*, 10 October.

Clark, Burton R 1998, *Creating entrepreneurial universities: organizational pathways of transformation*, IAU Press, Oxford, New York and Tokyo.

Chai Hon Chan 2002, advisor, World Bank, interview with author, 12 December.

Chia, Ying Lim 2003, 'Malaysian delegation heads to China for education mission', www.studymalaysia.com, 27 October.

Chin, Tarcisius 1994, 'Education industry'. *Far Eastern Economic Review*, 5 March.

Considine, Mark 1988, 'The corporate management framework as administrative science: a critique', *Australian Journal of Public Administration* XLVII(1).

Crouch, Harold 1996, *Government and society in Malaysia*, Allen & Unwin, Singapore.

Cummings, William K 1998, 'The third revolution of higher education: reaching out', Motohisa Kaneko (trans), *Koutou kyouiku kenkyu [Study of Higher Education]* 1.

Davis, Glyn 2002, 'A little learning? Public policy and Australian universities', lecture, Griffith University, 26 September.

Department of Statistics, Malaysia 1970, *Population and housing census of Malaysia: census classifications and the tabulation plan*. Government Printer, Kuala Lumpur.

Dill, David D and Barbara Sporn (eds) 1995, *Emerging patterns of social demand and university reform: through a glass darkly*, IAU Press, Oxford, New York and Tokyo.

DiMaggio, Paul J and Walter W Powell 1983, 'The iron cage revisited: institutional isomorphism and collective rationality in organizational fields', *American Sociological Review* 48(2).

*Education Quarterly* 2000, 'A century review', 8.

EPU (Economic Planning Unit) 1991, *Privatisation Masterplan*, Prime Minister's Department, Government Printer, Kuala Lumpur.

—— 1985, *Guidelines on privatisation*, Government Printer, Kuala Lumpur.

*FEER* (*Far Eastern Economic Review*) 2000, 'The tug of war for Asia's best brains', 9 November.

—— 2001, Country briefing, 22 November.

Funston, John, N 1980, *Malay politics in Malaysia: a study of the United Malays National Organization and Party Islam*, Heinemann Educational Books (Asia) Ltd, Kuala Lumpur, Singapore, Hong Kong.

Gale, Bruce 1981, *Politics and public enterprise in Malaysia*, Eastern Universities Press, Petaling Jaya.

Gomez, Edmund Terence 2003, Associate Professor, Department of Administrative Studies and Politics, Faculty of Economics and Administration, University of Malaya, 26 March.

Gomez, Gavin 2003, 'Less exam-centered system', the *Star*, 7 May.

Gopinathan, S 1995, 'Globalisation, the state and education policy in Singapore', paper presented at the *Globalisation and Learning* conference, New College, Oxford, September.

Hassan Karim and Siti Nor Hamid (eds) 1984, *With the people: the Malaysian student movement 1967–74*, Institut Analisa Sosial, Petaling Jaya.

Higashikawa, Shigeru 1996, 'Kokumin kaihatu keikaku (NDP) to minnkann kyouiku' [NDP and education] in Hara, Fujio and Takashi Torii (eds), *Kokumin kaihatu keikakukano mareshia* [*Malaysia at the time of NDP*], Institute of Developing Economies, Tokyo.

Hirschman, Charles 1979, 'Political independence and educational opportunity in peninsular Malaysia', *Sociology of Education* 52, April.

Indramalar, S 2003, 'Lower funding for varsities', *Study Guardian* 2(4).

Jomo, KS (ed) 1994, *Malaysia's economy in nineties*, Pelanduk Publication, Darul Ehsan.

JPM (Jabatan Perangkaan Malaysia [Department of Statistics]) 2001, *Buletin perangkaan sosial Malaysia 2001* [*Social Statistics Bulletin 2001*], Government Printer, Kuala Lumpur.

Kaur, Jeswant 2003, 'The problem with local grads...' *Sunday Mail*, 14 September.

Kerr, Clark 1995, *The uses of the university*, Harvard University Press, Cambridge and London.

Khattab, Umi 2002, 'Closing gaps between private, public varsities', *New Straits Times*, 5 October.

Kitamura, Kazuyuki 2001, *Gendai daigaku no henkaku to seisaku* [*Reform and policy of contemporary universities*], Tamagawa University Press, Tokyo.

Lam, Li 2003, 'Produce graduates who can work, says Fong', the *Star*, 30 June.

Lee, Molly NN 2001a, 'Educational reforms in Malaysia: global challenge and national response', paper presented at the International Forum on Educational

Reforms in the Asia-Pacific Region: Globalization, Localization, and Individualization for the Future, Hong Kong Institute of Education, 14–16 February.

—— 2001b, 'The corporatisation of a public university: influence of market forces and state control', paper presented at the Third International Malaysian Studies Conference, 6–8 August.

—— 2002a, 'Academic profession in Malaysia and Singapore' in Altbach, Philip G (ed), *The decline of the guru: the academic profession in developing and middle-income countries*, Center for International Higher Education, Boston.

—— 2002b, Associate Professor, School of Education, Universitie Sains Malaysia, interview with author, 18, 19 and 20 November.

—— 2004, 'Malaysian universities: towards equality, accessibility, and quality' in Altbach, Philip G and Toru Umakoshi (eds), *Asian universities: historical perspectives and contemporary challenges*, Johns Hopkins University Press, Baltimore.

—— no date, 'Quality management in a university', Advisory Committee to the Vice Chancellor, Universiti Sains Malaysia, Penang.

Leong, Nick 2003, 'NEAC proposes the creation of "super" varsity', the *Star Online*, http://thestar.com.my/, 12 June.

Liew, Lena 2003, 'Malaysian overseas education offices to be operational by October—Azhar', *Bernama*, 20 August.

Lim, Kit Siang 1997, 'University corporatization proposals should be underpinned by a through process of consultation with academicians to check serious brain drain in local universities', media statement, www.limkitsiang.com/archive/1997/Feb97/sg283.htm, 17 February.

—— 1999, 'Najib to be questioned in Parliament about the summary and arbitrary termination of Chandra as Director of the Centre for Civilisational Dialogues, University of Malaya', media statement, www.limkitsiang.com/archive/1999/feb99/sg1600.htm, 28 February.

Loh, Francis Koh Wah 1996, 'Corporatisation of the universities: the market to the rescue?', *Aliran Monthly*, 16(1).

Loh, Philip Fook Seng 1975, *Seeds of separatism: educational policy in Malaya 1874–1940*, Oxford University Press, Kuala Lumpur.

Mahathir Mohamad 1991, *Malaysia: the way forward*, speech presented at the inaugural meeting of the Malaysian Business Council, Kuala Lumpur, 28 February.

—— 2001, *The Third Outline Perspective Plan*, opening speech in parliament, 3 April.

Malaysia 1967, *Penyata Jawatan-Kuasa Peranchang Pelajaran Tinggi* [*Report of the Higher Education Planning Committee*] Government Printer, Kuala Lumpur.

—— 1996, *Seventh Malaysia Plan 1996–2000*, Government Printer, Kuala Lumpur.

—— 2001, *Eighth Malaysia Plan 2001–2005*, Government Printer, Kuala Lumpur.

Marginson, Simon and Mark Considine 2000, *The enterprise university: power, governance and reinvention in Australia*, Cambridge University Press, Cambridge.

Mauzy, Diane K 1985, 'Language and language policy in Malaysia' in Beer, William R and James E Jacob (eds), *Language policy and national unity*, Rowan & Allanheld, Totowa.

McMahon, Mary E 1992, 'Higher education in a world market: an historical look at the global context of international study', *Higher Education* 24

Milne, RS and DK Mauzy 1978, *Politics and government in Malaysia*, University of British Columbia, Vancouver.

—— 1999, *Malaysian politics under Mahathir*, Routledge, London.

Ministry of Education 2001, *Directory of higher education Malaysia*, third edition, Utsusan Publications and Distributions Sdn Bhd, Kuala Lumpur.

—— 2001, *Education in Malaysia: a journey to excellence*, Government Printer, Kuala Lumpur.

Mohamad, Yusri 1996, 'Lingering doubts', *Aliran* 16(1).

Muzaffar, Chandra 1999, 'Removal from the University of Malaya', *Berita Reformasi*, www.geocities.com/Tokyo/Flats/3797/eng0224c.htm

National Language Act 1967, Malaysia.

Neave, Guy and F van Vught 1994, *Government and higher education relationships across three continents: the winds of change*, IAU Press, Oxford, New York and Tokyo.

Netto, Anil 1999, 'Academics speak out at their own risk', *Inter Press Service*, 14 June.

Newman, John Henry 1976 [1852], *The idea of a university*, edited by Ker, IT, Clarendon Press, Oxford.

*New Straits Times* 1994, 'Plan to improve, expand scope of tertiary studies', 5 January.

—— 1996, 'Forging strong academia-industry ties', 8 September.

—— 2000, 'Unemployed Graduates', 3 August.

—— 2003, 'Universities of merit', 5 March.

Ng, Boey Kui 1998, 'The new economic policy and Chinese in Malaysia: impact and responses', *Journal of Malaysian Chinese Studies* 2(December).

Nik Aziz Nik Pa 2002, Dean, Faculty of Education, Universiti Malaya, interview with author, 5 December.

OECD (Organization for Economic Cooperation and Development) 1987, *Universities under scrutiny*, Paris.

Osman, Mohd Taib 2002, 'The ivory tower: some dimensions of organisational development' in Hussin, Sufean (ed), *Revitalising education: some prospective policy innovations*, Utsusan Publications, Kuala Lumpur.

Rashid, Abd Rahim Abd 2002, 'Politics of higher education in Malaysia: trends and issues' in Hussin, Sufean (ed), *Rivitalizing education: some prospective policy innovations*, Utusan Publications, Kuala Lumpur.

Razak, Mohd Najib Tun Abdul 1997, 'Malaysia as a regional centre of educational excellence' in Asian Strategy and Leadership Institute (ed), *Malaysia today: towards the new millennium*, ASEAN Academic Press, London.

Reid, Linda J 1988, *The politics of education in Malaysia*, Department of Political Science Monograph Series, University of Tasmania, Hobart.

*Reuters News* 1995, 'Malaysia cuts college years to ease labour pains', 17 August.

Roff, Margaret 1967, 'The politics of language in Malaya', *Asian Survey* VII(5).

Rothblatt, Sheldon 1995, 'An historical perspective on the university's role in social development' in Dill, David D and Barbara Sporn (eds), *emerging patterns of social demand and university reform: through a glass darkly*, IAU Press, Oxford, New York and Tokyo.

Salazar, Lorraine C 2004, 'The political economy of telecommunications reform in Malaysia and the Philippines', PhD dissertation, Australian National University, Canberra.

Shariff, Noraini 1995, 'Premier varsity's man of vision,' *New Straits Times*, 5 December.

Selvaratnam, Viswanathan 1989, 'Change admidst continuity: university development in Malaysia' in Altbach, Philip G and Viswanathan Selvaratnam (eds), *From dependence to autonomy*, Kluwer Academic Publishers, Dordrecht.

Shafie, Halim and P Manogran 1999, *MS ISO 9000: A practical guide for implementation in the Civil Service*, National Institute of Public Administration, Kuala Lumpur.

Shah, Mohd Hazim, KS Jomo and Phua Kai Lit 2002, *New perspectives in Malaysian studies*, Malaysian Social Science Association, Kuala Lumpur.

Singh, Jasbir Sarjit and Hena Mukherjee 1993, 'Education and national integration in Malaysia', *International Journal of Educational Development* 13(2).

Snodgrass, Donald R 1980, *Inequality and economic development in Malaysia*, Oxford University Press, Kuala Lumpur.

*Star Online* 2003a, 'Varsity sets up a holding company,' 26 May.

—— 2003b, 'All varsities 'need R&D grant', 13 June.

Stensaker, Bjorn and Jorunn Dahl Norgard 2001, 'Innovation and isomorphism: a case-study of university identity straggle 1969–1999', *Higher Education Policy* 42.

Suehiro, Akira 2000, *Catch-up gata kougyouka ron* [*The catch-up industrialisation theory*], Nagoya University Press, Nagoya, Japan.

Suffian bin Hashim, Tun Mohamed 1976, *An introduction to the constitution of Malaysia* (second edition), Government of Malaysia, Kuala Lumpur.

Swinnerton-Dyer, Sir Peter 1995, 'Shijyoukano takurami to daigakuhyouka' [Evaluation of universities and market policies] in Kaneko, Motohisa (ed), *Kinmirai no daigakuzou*, Tamagawa University Press.

Tan, Ai Mei 2001, *Malaysian private higher education*, ASEAN Academic Press, London.

—— 2002, interview with author, 10 December.

Tan, Liok Ee 1997, *The politics of Chinese education in Malaysia*, Oxford University Press, Kuala Lumpur.

Tham, Seong Chee 1979, 'Issues in Malaysian education: past, present, and future', *Journal of Southeast Asian Studies* 10(2).

Thomas, R Murray (ed) 1983, *Politics and education: cases from eleven nations*, Pergamon Press, Oxford.

Torii, Takashi 2001, 'Mareshia no kaihatsu senryakuto seiji hendou' [Development strategies and political transformation in Malaysia] in Suehiro, Akira and Susumu Yamakage (eds) *Ajia seiji keizai ron* [*Politics and economy in Asia*], NTT Publisher, Tokyo.

Trow, Martin 1972, 'The expansion and transformation of higher education', *International Review of Education* 18.

—— 1986, 'The state of higher education in the United States' in Cummings, WK, EK Beauchamp, S Ichikawa, VN Kobayashi and M Ushiogi (eds), *Educational politics in crisis: Japanese and American perspectives*, Praeger Publishers, New York, Westport and London.

UNESCO 1998, *World conference on higher education—higher education in the twenty-first century: vision and action*, Paris, 5–9 October.

Universities and University Colleges Act [Akta Universiti dan Kolej] (amendment) 1996. Act 946, Malaysia.

USM (Universiti Sains Malaysia) 2001, *Laporan Tahuan 2001* [*Annual Report 2001*], Universiti Sains Malaysia, Penang.

Wan Ahmad Kamil Mahmood 2002, Associate Professor, Director Corporate Development Division, Universiti Sains Malaysia, interview with author, 19 November.

Zainal Abidin Abdul Wahid [no date], 'Pendidikan bahasa dan masa depan Malaysia' [Language education and the future], paper presented to the National Association of Islamic Students and the Linguistics Association of Malaysia.